The Other Side of the Siderail

Memoirs of a Nurse Who Became a Patient

By **Donna Stapleton**

Lulu Publishing

This book is dedicated to the caregivers, to anyone who has ever held a hand or soothed the pain and fear of a scared and suffering person. Whether you are medically trained or simply a relative, friend, neighbor or bystander who answers the cry for help and comfort. Your actions and words mean so much more than you think.

Table of Contents

Chapter 1

Major

I was five years old when I realized that Medicine was my destiny. The circumstances of this revelation involved a painful incident that would ultimately change the course of my life. (Up until that fateful day my favored career choice was cowgirl).

My mother had warned me countless times to avoid stray dogs but some things just need to be learned on a first hand basis. Wandering around the front yard in search of a good rock for my collection, I felt a sudden thrill when I spied my neighbor's German Shepherd eating out of a garbage pail in another neighbor's driveway. Major was fairly new to the local menagerie of family pets and since he was usually chained in his own back yard, I had never had the opportunity to pet this magnificent specimen of furry wonder. Gingerly sidling up to him with a growing sense of excitement that he wasn't shying away at my approach, I ignored the ominous fact that a broken steel chain

1

dangled from his collar onto the ground beside him. I was going to get a chance to pet him! Nobody in the neighborhood had petted Major. Oh sure we had all petted the old tame Shepherd Blacky a million times. But Major was *new*. And I would be the first to meet him! So all bets were off as far as prior warnings or even simple common sense were concerned.

He never lifted his head from his garbage meal as I gently placed my hand upon his back but as I stroked him he began to vibrate and his hair rose up as if someone was inflating him. Thinking that he was frightened of me and mistaking the vibrations for trembling I began to croon softly as I continued to pet him. He set me straight a few moments later when he suddenly rose up from his makeshift meal and thrust his growling toothy snout in my face. Even a dumb five year old like myself could tell by his expression that he was definitely not in a petting mood. Coming to my senses a day late and a dollar short, I started to back up slowly while keeping an eye on that very pissed off countenance. I never knew a dog had that many teeth. And they were much larger than I remembered, especially considering the way that his lips were peeled back to make certain I could admire every single one of them. This was definitely one of the earliest memories that I have of hearing what I now think of as my inner voice. I'm not schizophrenic or anything but I do have this silent inner voice that reverberates within my skull from time to time. It is usually silently berating someone who is giving me a hard time or acting like an idiot. But this time it was aimed right back at me. *Donna you are one dumb shithead and why oh why couldn't you have stayed in the backyard with your Barbie dolls?* Actually I don't think my inner voice used the word "shithead" because I wasn't allowed to curse yet.

What happened next took place so rapidly that the motion is blurred in my mind but the visceral memory has persisted strongly enough to instill a lifelong fear of German Shepherds. (Luckily I am somehow able to separate them from other dogs so that my love of animals in general has not been affected). I got maybe a yard or two away before Major decided that I was more interesting than his garbage meal. Still facing him and too terrified to take my eyes off of him, I retreated more quickly until I was nearly running backwards. His advance toward me culminated in one of the most frightening moments in my life and even fifty years later, if I close my eyes, I can still see it in a sort of slow motion clip. He actually leapt through the air and took me down. I remember protectively raising my right arm to ward him off in an instinctive move that saved my face and throat. But he grabbed my arm in his feral jaws and started shaking it like a toy. I started kicking him with my right foot, an action that served only to have him turn his attention (and his teeth) to my right leg. The entire episode was accompanied by a frenzied sort of snarling growl that still has the power to terrify me into a state of immobility.

We had a collie that looked exactly like Lassie and she was very protective. Whether she could have prevailed against Major was to remain a mystery because she never showed up. My brother John saved my life that day. Hearing my screams from the back yard, he came to investigate. (My mother had also heard them but she came a lot slower since she was so used to hearing me scream for no reason.) Shuffling down the driveway dragging a cowboy rope behind him he called out, "What's a matta Donner?"

And just like that, at the sound of my brother's voice, Majors' homicidal rage was broken. He dropped my leg, threw my brother a baleful glare and slunk back to the garbage like nothing had ever happened.

Peeling my battered self off the ground I began to limp toward my brother just as my mother opened the front door. By that time my brother had sized up the situation and informed her, "Donna got bit by the dog."

Used to my daily display of dramatics (my childhood nickname was Sarah Bernhardt after a well-known actress from an earlier time), my mother proceeded to chastise me. "Good for you! How many times have I told you not to pet stray dogs?" (Today's indulgent Mothers might consider this to be a rather heartless rejoinder. It must be taken in the context of an era when the school principle could paddle your backside and that would most likely be followed by an additional spanking when you got home if your Mother found out about it.)

"It was Major, Mom." My brother informed her as she held the front door open for me and ushered me into the bathroom to clean my tearstained face and assess the damage. The assessment didn't last long. My Mother had been a WAC during World War II. That's where she met my Dad. When it came to weathering a storm, standing up for her rights or facing the challenges of life, my mother was one tough and wise woman but in the few major physical crises that occurred in my life, well, let's just say that heroics were not her forte. All I know is that one moment she was peeling back my sleeve to wash the blood away and the next she was gone, leaving me standing beside a sink of running bloodstained water. She was quickly replaced when a next-door neighbor took over the job of rinsing my wounds. I recall my Mother's friend calling out to my Mom who was standing in the next room, unable to bear the site of my torn flesh, "I keep finding more of them! We'd better get her to a doctor."

In those days most families in our middle class neighborhood had just one car and it was usually driven to work by the Dad while the mothers stayed at home and saw to the house and children. You didn't call an ambulance or go to an emergency room seeking a plastic surgeon for a few dog bites. But I needed more than a Band-Aid and as it happened, the only car to be found on our block belonged to Phil, the owner of the dog who had bit me. Phil was a Jew who had been in a concentration camp during the war. Overheard in whispered conversations were rumors of horrible events that he had suffered having to do with the deaths of his mother and sister. Whatever terrors he had endured had made him somewhat skittish, especially when it came to loud noises. My brother and I once saw him jump the fence and dive to the ground when an army plane came in low on its way to the local airport. His experiences also made him obsessed with acquiring a string of increasingly vicious German Shepherds. I wasn't Major's first victim. In fact, I learned that the dog had bitten two people before he sunk his teeth into me, making his latest attack a canine capital offense. (Apparently the law stated that three strikes and you're out when it comes to dogs biting people. Lucky it only applied to dogs. I knew a kid who used to bite everyone just for the fun of it.)

If I felt guilty that Major was to go to The Chamber because of me it has vanished from my memory. All I know is that the next dog Phil bought was even worse. They had to keep Prince in the garage and after owning him for just a few months the dog jumped clear through the garage window and attacked the paperboy who was riding his bicycle past the house.

Phil was the one who ultimately wrapped me in a blanket, loaded me into his car along with my mother and brother and drove us to our family doctor.

I was ushered right into a treatment room without having to wait in the waiting room and Phil placed me gently on an exam table. Moments later the doctor bustled in and in his unruffled manor he began to assess the extent of my wounds. There was actually an inch of fat hanging out of one of the ugliest wounds on my skinny little forearm and I couldn't imagine how he was going to fix *that*, but his confidence had a calming effect. I watched in growing interest as he sprayed some kind of foam on each of the wounds while quietly issuing orders to a nurse who was gathering supplies from a number of cabinets that lined the walls. To this day I don't know if that foam was an antiseptic or an anesthetic but I don't associate pain with what came next. It was the most amazing thing! That doctor took a needle and thread and started to sew me back together! I watched with growing admiration as he proceeded to close those hideous gaping wounds. They must have been pretty gory because having looked at them; my mother and brother had become woozy and were occupying their own exam tables in other rooms down the hall while I was being stitched back together.

Later on I was told that I got twenty-one stitches that day. Back then it was very important to know just how many stitches you got when you were injured. It was the first question people would ask you, right before asking if it hurt. "How many stitches did you get?" Occasionally a patient will ask me how many stitches they got in the course of their surgery. We don't actually count the stitches anymore although we do count the needles and instruments to make sure that we don't leave anything inside where it doesn't belong. You can make quite a few stitches with each needle. But twenty-one was the magic number for me that day in September of 1959 and that's what I proudly imparted to the other kids in the neighborhood as they questioned me about the sling supporting my right arm.

A decade later I was spending much of my spare time as a candy striper at the local hospital, an activity that ultimately led me to the profession of nursing. And despite having spent more than three decades of midnight shifts, missed Christmases and the physical toll paid for running to emergencies and standing on my feet for hours at a time, I have never regretted my choice. Nursing never was just something that I do for a living; it's what I am.

Empathy is a quality that is handed out to people in varying amounts. It can be blunted or tamped down through experience or by sheer will. It can also be selective. To wit, I can stick a needle into someone's flesh, hold pressure on a gaping wound and pose a dead baby for photographs but I can't stand to watch a boxing match on television. Healing, holding a scared or suffering person's hand, accompanying the afflicted on their journey, even if it involves being subjected to noxious smells or sights comes naturally to me. In the throes of pain and fear people can be less than grateful for even your best attempts at helping them. Throughout my career I have been bruised countless times by fingers squeezing my arms for comfort. I've also been kicked, slapped, bitten and threatened with homicidal intent. Vomit, spit, blood, feces, urine and various other bodily fluids have made their unctuous way onto my person. Most of my colleagues have had experiences similar to mine and yet they continue to render the tenderest care to their patients day after day and year after year. Empathy involves understanding that people behave differently when they are hurt and scared. The sheer loss of control over every aspect of your life during an illness or hospitalization is devastating. Your bodily functions become public and your body parts are commandeered by legions of hospital staff. Adrenaline shuts down large sections of the brain while other areas prepare for battle. A lifetime ago I was certain that a person couldn't go into the profession of nursing unless they understood these things. Unless they possessed an abundance of the empathy gene. I was wrong. Nurse Ratchet does exist. I met her. When I found myself on the other side of the siderail.

Chapter 2

Nurse Ratchet

Anyone who has ever seen *One Flew Over the Cuckoos Nest* will remember Nurse Ratchet as the cold and efficient charge nurse who managed to drive one of her young patients to commit suicide. Her complete lack of both empathy and remorse have marked her as the epitome of the hardened, jaded clinically efficient nurse who is all business but lacking in all human empathy. The name is a synonym for coldhearted and callous, the last traits that you wish to see in the person upon whom your health and welfare depends when you are most vulnerable.

My first introduction to Nurse Ratchet occurred when my father was a patient. Healthy as a horse for the first six decades of his life, Dad became wheelchair bound at the age of seventy-six after a devastating stroke. His initial hospitalization in mid-December of 1990 was extended through Easter weekend due to a fractured hip sustained in the Institute For Rehabilitation at Brunswick Hospital in Amityville, Long Island.

Yes, it was *that* Amityville, and our once robust family underwent its' own little horror. Over the course of the next seven years he was hospitalized countless times for various ailments, nearly always at the same institution where I was employed. Evidently the compassionate care that I had given to my patients over the preceding years left no ready supply of benevolence in the bank for my kin or me.

Paralysis of his left arm and residual weakness in his left leg made independent mobility out of the question for my father. Consequently a bathroom trip translated into a slow, shuffling procession accompanied by a person on one side and a walk cane on the other for balance. Coupled with the vagaries of an elderly prostate gland this could have made my mother's life a sleepless hell. But her enterprising genius led to her hanging several hand-held plastic urinals on the siderail of Dad's home hospital bed, each with a bit of toilet tissue and a hand wipe, that could be emptied during her own nocturnal visits to the bathroom. Dad was a fastidious gent who never spilled a drop in seven years as long as the urinals were left in place. His single incidence of incontinence occurred during the initial stroke when he was semiconscious. But his perfect record was broken when he ran up against Nurse Ratchet on the Forth Floor.

My scheduled time to work was about to begin soon after one of Dad's hospital admissions and I hesitated to leave him. But he was stable and I had become a veteran of Dad-crises. So I assured him that I would return on my break in a few hours and, after repeating instructions to the nurse about the necessity of leaving the urinals on the siderail, I hurried off to my unit to change into scrubs for my shift. Of course any nurse will tell you that the worst time to pass on information or instructions is at change-of-shift. That's the time when the outgoing staff, exhausted from the day's events, is giving report to the oncoming nurses and hoping that they have remembered to impart all critical information. It's a particularly stressful time of day (or night) and heaven help the patient who codes (has a cardiac arrest) at change-of shift, let alone a bathroom emergency.

When I returned a few hours later, my father had been moved to a room remote from the nurses station. He had a window spot in the semi-private space and was alone in the room with the curtain pulled, blocking him from view by anyone passing by his remote corner of the unit.

"Girl", he whispered to me in a desperate plea, employing the nickname he had called me since I was his little girl, "I pissed the bed!" His panicked countenance will haunt me for as long as I live. He was not only uncomfortable in his cold and damp nest of urine-soaked sheets; he was mortified. His cheeks were flushed and sweat had broken out on his forehead. This brave, strong willed man was on the verge of tears. "I kept ringing and calling out but nobody came!" A quick glance around the room revealed that the urinals I had left on his siderail were gone. A single urinal rested uselessly on a table against a far wall, well out of reach. Tamping down my trembling rage in an effort to preserve his dignity I calmly patted his back.

"It's okay Pop. Not a problem. Not your fault. I'll be right back and you'll be all cleaned up in a jiffy."

I was actually afraid that in my building fury I might say or do something that might end with me being physically restrained. I didn't want his embarrassment witnessed by the nursing staff, and I also harbored a suspicion that no one could take care of my Dad as well as I could. Dealing with his infirmity in the preceding years had allowed us to develop the ability to allow my assistance in his toiletry without interfering with his dignity. I had, after all, taken him on dozens of field trips to shopping centers, fishing boats and workshops where it was necessary for me to accompany him to the men's room.

Approaching the nurses' station, I managed to calmly request direction to the linen closet. Peering at me from behind her glasses the nurse inquired, "What do you need Hun?"

Taking a deep breath I replied, "I need some clean sheets and towels and a new gown."

"For who?"

"For my father," my teeth were clenched by this point.

"Oh. He soiled himself?" she inquired with a supercilious curl of her hairy lip.

My jaw dropped. I was speechless for a moment. "I specifically left instructions that the urinals were to be left on my father's siderail" I finally gasped. "Not only were they removed, he wasn't given a call bell and the one urinal left in the room was out of his reach. He's *paralyzed*." I spoke now to her back as she preceded me down the hall to his room.

Not wanting to cause a scene in front of my father, I quietly pointed to the urinal that was resting several feet out of reach. She looked from the urinal to my father and back again.

"He must have moved it there." She concluded.

Incredulous, I couldn't even voice a protest. Even my inner voice was shocked into silence. A paralyzed man who can't get out of bed to pee got out of bed to move his urinal out of reach and then climbed back over the siderail so that he could pee the bed and wallow in urine until his daughter arrived? Bingo. Makes perfect sense.

"Look. All I need are the sheets." At her skeptical look I assured her, "I'm a nurse. I work here. Just tell me where your linen closet is."

Pulling the curtain closed in my face she replied, "Well then, if you work here, you know that you're not allowed to help. (I knew no such thing but again, I didn't want to make a scene and embarrass my father further.) "Have a seat over there. I'll clean him up."

Nearly choking on my tongue, I took a seat near the doorway and began to plot how I would murder this unfeeling scumbag in the parking lot after work despite the fact that I am a nonviolent pacifist. Within minutes she came to stand nearly on top of me in the doorway so that she could call out to her coworkers down the hall, "I need some help in here."

That nurse exemplified the epitome of how not to treat people. She was a cruel, uncaring and unfeeling control freak Nazi Nurse and I have met many others just like her since that day. One was riding shotgun over visiting passes for a dying relative in the ICU. Another one rolled her eyes in front of a patient I was transferring to another unit and complained loudly in front of the patient, "Another patient? That's not fair. I've already had four admissions and you're dumping another one on me?!!" Then there was the unfeeling gargoyle of a clipboard-wielding nursing supervisor who flippantly remarked to a coworker that the patients were dropping like flies that night. I was standing only a few yards away and easily overheard her comment. Only minutes before, a cardiac arrest team had swarmed off of the elevator with the internal defibrillator paddles. My mother was the only one on the table in the Cardiac Cath Lab that night. The doctor hadn't yet emerged to tell me but that was how I learned of my mother's death.

18

The Nurse Ratchet experiences that I endured throughout my parent's elder years made me a scalpophobe, to use a word that I coined in a humorous attempt to describe my resistance to all medical interventions on my person. I was fifty before I went for my first Mammogram and I still haven't submitted to a colonoscopy despite repeated recommendations by both the medical community at large and my personal physician. I don't think that I'm unique in this proclivity. Many doctors and nurses shy away from standard medical treatment. My Labor and Delivery colleagues are among the worst for disregarding the need for regular Pap smears and GYN exams. (Would you take your clothes off and allow your coworkers intimate access to your person?) My gynecologist is my age and he hasn't gone for his first colonoscopy either. We ride each other about it whenever we see each other. Okay, I'll go if you go...

My first mammogram experience only reinforced my aversion to medical procedures performed upon my person. A week after undergoing the excruciating experience of having my poor breasts squished into pancakes by a cold, unyielding machine wielded by an equally cold operator, I received a phone call that I needed to return for a repeat mammogram because something on the film required further investigation. I was also to obtain a prescription from my gyno for a sonogram and fine needle biopsy if needed. Jeez. I knew I should never have opened this can of worms in the first place. My breasts were just fine until they got crushed! I called a friend, a radiology tech who worked in the radiology center where my mammogram had been done and arranged to have my rerun when she could be there for moral support. "Don't worry," she reassured me, "They always call you back the first time- there's nothing to reference it to. Probably nothing."

From your mouth to God's ear, I thought.

My friend met me in the waiting room and led me back to the changing room and then the mammo room, where my prior film was hanging on the wall.

"See this is what they want to look at." She pointed to a tiny pea-shaped white spot on the right upper side of my left breast. "It probably won't even be there today. And if it is they'll just do a sono. But it's probably nothing; happens all the time."

She then placed my left breast back in the torture machine and proceeded to reshape my breast into a form it did not wish to take. Then she gave me a hug and led me back out to the waiting room.

"It will just be a few minutes; I'll make sure Doc looks at them right away and then you can go. Don't worry. I'm sure it will be fine." God Bless her she made the fear that I was trying so hard to fight seem bearable.

Then about twenty minutes later she returned to the waiting room with a look of concern on her face and said that I needed to have a sonogram for further investigation; the spot in the medial area of my right breast was still there. My heart plummeted to my toes as I stood up and followed her into a small dark room and was placed in a semi-reclining chair to await the sono technician. After a few minutes she entered and, after scanning my chart, advised me to raise my left arm over my head. She then took the gel-covered sono wand and began circling it around my left armpit while peering at the screen in concentration.

"So you're a friend of Dana's?" she asked with a smile. I nodded in the affirmative. "Don't worry," she kindly reassured me. This always happens the first time. I'm sure it's nothing." After a few minutes of prowling around the outer edge of my left breast she suddenly leaned back and smiled, shaking her head while she wiped off the gel from the wand with a cloth.

"Those are just fluid-filled cysts," she breezily announced with a shake of her head. "Nothing to worry about".

I stared at her in consternation. She hadn't even scanned the part of my breast that held the suspicious little pea. "It's medial," I stated.

"Huh?" she inquired.

"It's medial," I repeated, using the medical term that denotes the side closest to the center of the body as opposed to the term lateral, which would mean toward the side. She had been scanning the lateral edge of my breast. What are you a dipshit, I thought? And where did you get your license?

She peered at me with a confused look until finally the light bulb came on. "Ooooooooh! Damn!," she said with a self-conscious shrug. "I always get that mixed up. Then she re-gelled the wand and returned it to my left breast, this time in the appropriate right side. After a moment, she leaned forward and peered closely at the screen and then shot a picture through the sono machine. Her eyes seemed to widen in concern. Then she wiped off the wand and, refusing to make eye contact with me, informed me not to move and said that the doctor would attend me shortly. Then she briskly exited the room.

For the next two hours, or maybe it was only twenty minutes, I laid there in the darkness with my left arm curled over my head and began to plan my funeral. The serious concerned look upon her face could only translate into doom. The doctor, a stout but diminutive transplant with an accent that evoked the Middle East finally bustled in and grabbed the wand after rapidly introducing herself. Leaning towards the screen with her eyebrows pressed together in concentration, she explored my left breast, this time the medial aspect.

Not a minute later she proficiently wiped the wand clean and stated, "Okay you can go. You should return in six months." Then she exited the room in a hurried flutter of white lab coat and medical adroitness without pausing a moment for explanation or encouragement.

I sat there for a moment with my arm still looped over my head. What the hell just happened? And does anyone still wonder why I don't pursue the recommended preventive care? Pavlov's dog had nothing on me. This girl has been trained…

Yes, Nurses are not the only Health Care Professionals who can be heartlessly cold or cruel. During another one of my father's post-stroke hospital admissions I was initially relieved when one of the most respected surgeons at my hospital operated after several days of watching my Dad lay in bed with a tube down his nose in an attempt to alleviate his abdominal discomfort and vomiting. The surgeon informed me that they had operated just in time. My father's gallbladder had been so diseased that it probably would have killed him if they had waited any longer. A long, angry incision ran vertically the entire length of Dad's abdomen, criss-crossed with large retention sutures, but I was grateful that he was still alive. A few weeks later I wheeled Dad into the Doctor's office for a follow-up visit with the surgeon's partner who had assisted on the case.

"Good thing you operated in time, huh?," I said. "I heard his gallbladder was ready to explode."

"There was nothing wrong with his gallbladder." The surgeon replied with a sarcastic grin.

"But Doctor ... told me his gallbladder was rancid."

"Well I guess he felt that he had to say something." He smirked. "He couldn't very well say that we couldn't find a damn thing wrong inside there."

I was speechless. In fact I think even my inner voice was speechless. Who was lying? And even if the first surgeon, who was the Chief of Surgery and practically worshipped as a local God was lying, what was the point in his partner telling me that my Dad had just suffered through a painful, life-threatening surgery for virtually no reason?

Another negative incident involved a P.A. (Physician's Assistant) at the Brunswick Center for Rehabilitation where my Dad was transferred after his stroke. After nearly two months of intensive inpatient therapy, Dad was nearly ready to come home at last. I arrived with my Mom the evening before his scheduled discharge to find my father sitting in a chair beside the bed along with my brother John who had come to visit. John and hospitals, or any type of blood or bodily fluids, smells or byproducts, whether they are actually encountered or even just mentioned at a dinner table conversation, do not get along very well. He's a brave guy who will stand up to someone twice his size and I believe that he would give me the shirt off of his back if I needed it, but he has been known to pass out at the sight of a cut on his finger.

I sat beside Dad and was in the process of discussing tomorrow's journey home when I saw from the corner of my eye a drop of blood as it hit the floor below my father's chair. Following it to the source I was concerned to see a cut on Dad's elbow that was oozing the bright red stuff. I popped up and headed for door to get help only to be snatched back into the room by my father's impassioned plea.

"Girl! Come back here!"

I turned in confusion at the obvious distress in his voice after I had summoned a nurse.

"Snitch!" he said.

I was quite unused to being reprimanded by him in such a manner. "Dad, what happened? Did you fall?" As the nurse entered the room I glanced toward my brother and noted his green complexion.

"He wanted to go to the bathroom and told me that he wanted me to help him and we didn't need the nurse," my brother said. "He was fine 'till halfway back but then he fell and he made me pick him up and put him in the chair. He wouldn't let me call the nurse."

My brother is strong and wiry but my Dad was easily half a head taller and at least fifty pounds heavier. It must have been an heroic feat, hefting him off of the floor and into the chair. My heart went out to John. He was rarely able to overcome his aversion long enough to visit Dad in the hospital and now the one time he did, he found himself in a lose-lose situation, torn between guilt and anxiety and my father's obvious stricture to keep mum about the episode. And my father's aversion to calling for help was suddenly clear. Over the preceding weeks my independent-minded, strong willed Dad had attempted to get out of bed without help several times and subsequently fallen more than once. I had noted bruises and scrapes from these mishaps that sometimes led to the application of a posy restraint, a vest-like garment that is attached to a chair in order to keep a patient from getting up. Restraints are sometimes used as a threat by unfeeling staff members. He was afraid that he would get in trouble and be punished for his fall.

The nurse had now arrived and after being apprised of the situation, insisted that my father be returned to bed for an examination. Between the two of us we had just managed to settle him back into a supine position when he let out a quiet groan and I felt my insides twist as his left leg began to shorten into an externally rotated position. A Classic and unmistakable Sign.

"Oh my God," I whispered in despair. "His hip is broken."

The nurse looked at me and then asked my father if his leg hurt. After his negative response she replied, "Look. I think he's fine but I'll call the P.A. to examine him."

Within minutes a young P.A. arrived and asked us to step outside a moment so that he could check my Dad. My Mom was starting to look so upset that I began to worry that we might have to find a bed for her soon. A short while later the P.A. emerged to tell us that Dad was fine; he only needed a band-aid for the elbow and he would be good as new.

Mom elbowed me in the side with a grunt of displeasure mixed with relief. "See, he's fine! Why did you have to be a Calamity Jane and get everyone all upset?"

This was starting to feel like an episode of *The Twilight Zone* to me. Who

were they going to believe, this young
P.A. or me? I had been a nurse for about
sixteen years at that time and seen more
than my share of broken hips when I
worked on a surgical unit in Manhattan.
I was also involved in training
Paramedics and EMTs. I knew what a
damned broken hip looked like.

"I want an X-Ray." I stood my
ground.

With a superior sigh of infinite
patience the P.A. nodded to the nurse
and my wish was granted even as Mom
threw her hands up in disbelief at my
stubbornness. They popped Dad onto a
stretcher as the P.A. left to attend to
things more suited to his valuable time
and the rest of us retreated to the
waiting room. After about half an hour
they returned Dad to his bed. We were
standing at his bedside when several
doctors appeared, including the Director
of the Rehabilitation wing where Dad
had been living the past two months.
Since this was a Sunday it was an
ominous sign that so much brass had
been collected to attend my father.

"Mr. Bartolillo," the good doctor
began. "I'm sorry to tell you that you
have broken your hip. It can be repaired
but you are going to need surgery in
order to remove the broken bone and
insert a prosthetic hip joint."

Well blow me over with a feather…

After a short pause Dad shook his head. "No I don't think I want to do that."

The doctor, a quiet and dignified Asian who I had respected until that moment surrendered with a sigh. "Very well. The alternative would be for you to lie flat in bed for about six weeks and see if it can heal that way."

My father nodded an affirmative to that idea while Mom heaved a sigh of relief. I was busy unlocking my jaw, which had frozen in disbelief. Was he kidding? He wasn't going to work a little to convince Dad to have the surgery?

"Dad," I broke in before the docs could leave the room. I felt like I was lost at sea and the lifeboats were drifting away into the fog. "Wait a minute. You have to think about this."

At my pleading look the Director nodded and said he would wait outside and give us a few minutes to discuss our options. Mom balked at the idea of surgery for Dad. Hadn't he been through enough? Why put him through more?

This is when I made one of the most difficult decisions in my life. Mom, Dad and my brother were against the operation. If I pushed it and he died in surgery, I would have to shoulder the blame for the rest of my life. But earlier in my nursing career I had seen what happens when you keep someone who has suffered a fractured hip on strict bedrest. Prior to the 1970's when hip replacement surgery became widespread, a broken hip in an elderly person was a death sentence. If they didn't die of pneumonia, they became septic from an infection of the bedsores sustained by lying in bed as their muscles atrophied or deadly blood clots formed in their blood vessels. Dad had already suffered from aspiration pneumonia in the hospital after his stroke and he was in a weakened condition. No way could he survive six weeks or more of strict bedrest. I sat down on the bed beside him and took his large hand in mine. "Dad, what's going on? Why don't you want to have the surgery?"

"I don't know. It makes me think of making soup, taking my bone out like that. I just don't like the idea."

Not the answer I had expected and I hardly knew how to respond but I would give it the old college try. "Look Dad," I said. "I'm asking you to trust me on this one. It's an easy surgery; piece of cake. You'll be up and walking tomorrow afternoon. If you stay in this bed…well. You might not make it. I'm asking you please to say yes. Do it for me."

I waited for what seemed like an eternity while he searched my eyes for an answer and battled his own internal demons. Finally he nodded his assent. Yessssss. Before he could change his mind I got the doctors back into the room, the consents for the surgery were signed and my father was transferred to the general hospital building across the way. I blocked out the vibes of trepidation emanating from my mother and brother while trying to keep both of them calm and upbeat. In the end, it *was* a piece of cake. Dad was walking, or at least standing to transfer into a chair, by the next afternoon just hours after surgery. In less than a week he was transferred back to the Center for Rehabilitation for another six weeks of rehab before we finally got to take him home.

I never saw that P.A. again, although I did ask a friend about him, another P.A. who sometimes worked at that hospital. It's not that I hold any ill will against him. But I have had moments when I fantasized about giving him a lecture on the signs and symptoms of a fractured hip.

I don't mean to imply that I think all health care workers are heartless and sadistic or just plain dumb. While the very nature of the medical professions demand some suppression of feeling in order to allow us to perform some of our tasks, from starting an IV to cutting someone open in an operating room or telling an old friend that they have an incurable illness, I have witnessed countless acts of kindness and compassion that go beyond the expectations of the situation. Nurses crying in the arms of a patient whose baby was born too soon to survive. Doctors and nurses attending the funeral of a child whose death they were unable to predict or prevent. Most of the people I work with have put their own lives in danger countless times in the performance of their work and they will continue to do so every day. It is understood and accepted that our career puts us on the frontlines of exposure to every deadly pathogen from HIV to the next germ warfare invention. I stood by after an Obstetrician I work with took a load of amniotic fluid square in the face. I offered to take over while he cleaned off his face and changed but he simply asked me to wipe his eyes (he didn't want to contaminate his sterile gloves) and then proceeded with the delivery, smiling the entire time and then congratulating the parents afterward although he had to have been cringing within. And stress? A single little mistake and someone can *die* because you weren't paying attention or you weren't quick enough or smart enough or you needed to pee. The profession does take a toll and the necessary deadening of feeling can unfortunately expand into a primal loss of humanity. For some, the rendering of care is ultimately distilled into a cold list of tasks to be performed within a strict and sterile time frame. The patient becomes naught but a burden who may be placing more than the allotted amount of demands upon your time. The flames of anger fired by long hours in a physically and emotionally taxing environment, forced overtime and short staffing need to be directed somewhere. The patient is a most convenient and helpless target.

There is a bumper sticker that I once saw on a social media application geared towards nurses. It consisted of a photograph of a call bell with a warning underneath, "This is not a toy." Nearly every nurse who has been in practice for a while has had a patient who abuses the call bell. But when you start dreaming of wrapping the wire around a patient's neck, maybe it's time to take a break. And time to remember why you chose to practice medicine in the first place.

Nurses are not the only medical professionals at risk for developing a Ratchet personality. Many physicians develop an emotionless and untouchable persona in an attempt to distance themselves from the predicaments of their clientele. Patients die. Even the really nice ones. Doctors will make mistakes in the course of their career and some of those mistakes will have permanent and potentially devastating consequences. Sometimes they will devote every ounce of their energy, skill and knowledge to a case, staying up all night at a patient's bedside while pursuing and perhaps even winning the best possible outcome with the zeal of a super-hero, only to have the patient turn around and sue. A malpractice lawsuit doesn't have to be successful to have an effect on the psyche of the person being sued. There is a sense of betrayal when the person you have cared for turns around and hauls you into court. Not to mention the legal fees, time spent away from your work and family as well as a possible increase in malpractice insurance costs. And you can't even predict the ones

who will sue. I have witnessed
situations where a practitioner was so
inept, cavalier or reckless that he should
have had his pants sued off but his
patients send a thank-you gift instead.
And I have seen the most dedicated
physicians who went the extra mile,
fought the good fight and did
everything right get dragged into court.

Every nurse has known a few
Doctor Ratchets; physicians who are
nasty or condescending to both the
nursing staff and their patients. Doctors
who are more rough than is necessary or
so cold or brisk when imparting
potentially devastating news that it
becomes difficult to believe that there is
still a human being within that
hardened shell. This callous disregard is
a blight upon the medical community
and causes more damage to the health
and welfare of the population than most
people realize. Early treatment and
preventative care is now recognized as
one of the most cost saving ways to
preserve health. The fear and pain of a
visit to the doctor or a hospital stay can
be mitigated by the presence of a caring
nurse or doctor, making it more likely
that the patient will return and follow
recommendations. But when the trauma
of the incident is compounded by a
heartless interaction with a doctor or

nurse, John Doe is likely to wait until his leg is falling off before he sees a doctor again.

Chapter 3

MDs, DOs, Chiropractors and Witch Doctors

Compounding the abuse of the Ratchets of the world is the existence of a great deal of professional competition and rivalry as well as arrogance in the medical profession and allied health fields. For example, many medical doctors and osteopaths will roll their eyes if you mention the fact that you went to a chiropractor for treatment. This is ludicrous when you consider the history of the various branches of medicine.

Several years ago the hospital where I work became affiliated with the New York School of Osteopathic Medicine (NYCOM). Historically there was a great deal of competition and even ill will between Osteopaths (D.O.'s), Chiropractors and Allopaths (aka Medical Doctors or M.D.'s). In the not so distant past Medical Doctors were still treating their patients with such drastic measures as cupping (placing burning hot cups on the back) and bleeding. Bleeding was accomplished with the use of leeches or lancets or sharp knives that were used to sever a vein in the inside surface of the arm in order to drain blood. Born from this questionable history, *Lancet* is the name of a prominent British medical journal. There was very little science and even less oversight involved in the medical profession.

Osteopathy, a means of treatment that involves manipulation of the bones, was invented in the 19th century by a Midwesterner named Andrew Taylor Still. He was actually an Allopathic doctor who had become disgusted with the harmful practices (and lack of success) of his colleagues. Around the same time, Daniel David Palmer, a Canadian grocer who settled in Iowa, invented Chiropractic. (Notice how using all three names makes them sound sinister? Sort of like Lee Harvey Oswald or John Wilkes Booth?) Unlike Andrew Still, Palmer had never been formally trained in medicine. But his success in treatment garnered his method a popularity that still irks many medical doctors today.

Over time, Medical Doctors managed to clinch the respectability award and as medicine became the lucrative industry that it is today the Osteopaths (D.O.'s) drifted closer to the Allopathic court. Osteopathic schools still offer training in bone manipulation but otherwise their training and abilities are virtually identical to those of an M.D. In fact, very few osteopaths choose to perform osteopathic manipulations or treatments and most will say they "aren't good at it" or "don't remember how to do it", even if they are interns straight out of medical school. Meanwhile, Chiropractors have been left on the fringe of modern medicine next to the acupuncturists and Reiki masters. But due to their popularity (and the success of their treatment?) most medical plans cover chiropractors the same as they would a medical doctor. As far as I was concerned, if the treatment did not involve needles or surgery and made me feel better in the bargain I was climbing on board.

For over twenty years I had known that I had degenerative osteoarthritis. As opposed to rheumatoid arthritis or other autoimmune joint diseases, osteoarthritis is a "wear and tear" disease. My first bout with arthritis occurred in my mid-twenties as a result of spending too many hours on horseback. Seen in the Emergency Room when I was unable to abduct my right hip (and therefore ride my horse), I was told that I had "stress" arthritis and should leave off riding for a few weeks until the joint calmed down. More than a decade later I was diagnosed and treated by both an orthopedist and a popular chiropractor that ministered to many of the hospital employees. The orthopedist injected medication directly into my back and right hip (with a *very* long needle) and the chiropractor treated me with massage, heat and manipulation. The treatments worked and within a few weeks I was as good as new.

Every five or six years I experienced a flare-up and I would need to return for a month or so of chiropractic treatment with an occasional Motrin thrown in for good measure. By 2008, I had moved too far a distance away from my first chiropractor to make frequent office visits convenient and my orthopedist had passed away from cancer. So I made an appointment with a chiropractor in my new neighborhood and started treatment several times a week.

The style of treatment in my new Chiropractor's office was gentler than I was used to. There was almost no cracking or twisting of my neck. In addition to chiropractic treatment, I was trying to stay healthy by remaining active. In the good weather I played tennis either with friends or in a league. There was also a gym in my apartment complex that I frequented on most of my days off. It was hard to avoid since I'm right across from the clubhouse and its appearance, visible from my kitchen window (and refrigerator door) would scold me into motion when I was feeling lazy. My usual ritual wasn't overly strenuous; a 35-minute cardio on the bicycle occasionally followed by a short engagement with the limited assortment of weight machines. As long as I worked up a sweat I was satisfied. One night in mid December I found the workout harder than usual. I double-checked the settings on the bicycle. It was set for the usual cardio routine, my pulse was in the target range and the red bars on the screen were no higher than usual. But my legs told me a different story; it was abnormally difficult to pedal.

I passed off the bicycle episode as a machine malfunction or a sign that I might need to step up my workout. It wasn't until the next morning that I realized my weakness on the bicycle was not just an isolated incident; there was something seriously wrong.

Chapter 4

<u>Keanu Reeves in a White Coat</u>

After watching my Dad endure the effects of a major stroke I was very aware that a person's life could change drastically in an instant. You could be healthy and on top of the world one minute and the next you could be sitting in a wheelchair completely dependent on other people for every single aspect of your existence. I knew it could happen. I just didn't know it could happen to me.

The existence of a major problem became glaringly obvious shortly after my feet touched the floor the morning after the stationary bicycle incident. The feeling in my thighs reminded me of the way I felt after a full day of snow skiing. Gliding down a slope in the last run of the day, I would experience such a rubbery feeling in my legs that I wasn't sure if I would be able to negotiate the turns needed to return me to the lodge in one piece. The same feeling is obtainable by riding a horse for two hours straight after not climbing into a saddle for a year. I was a frequent victim of this sort of weekend warrior activity. The only problem was that this time I had done nothing overly physical to bring about this level of debilitating weakness in my legs. My usual exercise bicycle routine was the only exertion I had undertaken in the past week.

I needed an answer and I needed it fast because I was scheduled to work that day. Over the course of my twenty-seven year employment at the hospital where I worked, I had almost never called in sick. This would prove to be a major benefit since I had acquired over three months of unused sick time. Out of some overzealous inner concept of a work ethic it was difficult for me to call in sick. But the weakness in my legs was terrifying and I made the call to work and then scheduled an appointment with my doctor.

Two of my colleagues had been diagnosed with Multiple Sclerosis over the course of the past year and the possibility that I had become the third victim was swirling around in my head. Other equally horrendous possibilities raced through my mind as I awaited my afternoon doctor's appointment. Along with the possible diagnoses were thoughts of both the prognoses and the current treatment modalities. The bane of having some grasp of medical knowledge is a continually worsening list of possible diseases to match your symptoms. When my children were small they could never complain of a headache without receiving a neurological exam to rule out meningitis. I checked for the rebound abdominal tenderness common in appendicitis if they had a bellyache. As an end result they learned not to make a big deal about not feeling well. They both have great work ethics and neither one complains overmuch about being sick or calls in sick to work on a whim.

After performing a physical exam my doctor asked me what I thought was the cause of my current condition. (He's an extremely intelligent physician with an unusual personality and I often feel like I'm either being lectured to or tested by a professor when I visit him.) "MS?" I tentatively offered.

"Well I would say that you're too old for MS", he responded. (There was an additional blah blah blah about viral or bacterial neuropathy after that but I didn't pay attention because my brain was stuck on the "too old" part. I'm only fifty-four for Christ's sake. Do I really look that old? Crap he looks older than me. Harrumph.) He then proceeded to write a prescription for a bunch of bloodwork and negotiated an appointment with a neurologist in two days.

I know that it would have taken much longer to get an appointment with the neurologist on my own, but still the next two days felt more like two years. I certainly couldn't go to work. My feet became increasingly numb and I developed what I can only describe as a duck-like walk. By the time I entered the neurology office I was also experiencing a burning pain across my left deltoid and stiffness in my fingers. Typing had become difficult and I was relegated to using the two-finger method.

I had to fill out a wad of paper work before seeing the neurologist. Listed first on my medical history was the osteoarthritis in my neck and hip. My otherwise healthy medical history included little more than eye surgery as a child and surgery for a broken wrist sustained over twenty years before when my horse fell.

Imagine my surprise when Keanu Reeves entered the room. Or at least, it could have been his double. Longish dark hair, jeans, surfer-dude posture and accent. During the course of the physical exam it was discovered that my left patellar (knee) reflex was hyperactive and my right patellar reflex was gone, a scary finding to me that the doctor responded to with the words, "Hmmm. That's puzzling."

'That's *puzzling*?' I thought. 'Are you freaking kidding me???!!! If *you* don't know what it means than what the hell am *I* supposed to do? Dude!'

My remarks were not actually uttered aloud. I have the misfortune to be pathologically non-confrontational and rarely verbalize the thoughts that are screaming inside my head. I think of it as my inner voice. I can carry on an entire conversation without making a sound. Oh sometimes there might be a damning look or two, a raised brow or even an understated shoulder shrug, but rarely is an actual word shared with the perpetrator of my angst. This form of communication is not recommended in current society and rarely achieves results. Actually it never achieves results since the receiver of the communiqué is usually unaware that he or she has been spoken to. But I was raised to be *so* polite.

The neurologist retreated from the exam room after instructing me to change back into my clothes and meet him in his office down the hall. In his office he looked up from my chart and began to question me about my impending divorce, offering the opinion that it was a difficult experience and questioning how I was dealing with the stress. I glanced at the letterhead on the prescription pad he was clutching while my inner voice said, "Neurologist, right? Not psychiatrist? Does he think this is all in my mind? A psychosomatic illness?"

I offered the information as stated on my history that I had been taking Wellbutrin for several months. I had really been taking the antidepressant medication to help me quit smoking without gaining weight. He then gave me several samples of an alternative antidepressant and a prescription for both the drug and a long list of bloodwork.

"Do you think that the Wellbutrin is causing this?" I asked with a skeptical crinkling of my brows. (This was said by my actual voice, not my inner voice).

"Well, we have to cover all the bases." he replied before escorting me out to the waiting room to schedule my next appointment. "What kind of insurance do you have?" he questioned. "I'd also like you to have an MRI of the brain. You might need authorization." According to the receptionist, I should call in a few days to find out if the MRI had been authorized and return in a month for a follow-up visit. "A month?" My inner voice went into overdrive at that news as I cycled through all of the ramifications. "I can't be sick for a month!" it screamed as I left the office. "I have to work tomorrow!"

Chapter 5

<u>Doesn't Anybody Know What They're Doing?</u>

I didn't become afraid of needles until nursing school. I suppose it was the realization that many of my fellow students and later some of my colleagues didn't *know what the hell they were doing* that fostered not only my fear of needles but a distrust of medical personnel in general. The fact that I readily offered up my arm to the phlebotomist for bloodletting was a measure of the apprehension I was feeling about my worsening symptoms. Not a single moan, tear or pulling back from the needle. (In fact, the girl was quite skilled and I barely felt the needle as she withdrew over ten tubes of blood from my right arm.) I was quite proud of myself.

I dutifully called the neurology office several days later to find out if my MRI had been authorized and to obtain the results of my blood tests. The secretary informed me that the doctor had not yet dictated his notes and would be off the rest of the week so I would have to wait. To this day I have no idea what dictating notes has to do with obtaining an authorization for an MRI. All it takes is a damn phone call. But the office person to whom I spoke was adamant. I made it through the weekend supported by phone calls from my friends at work. When Monday came, I again called the neurology office and was again informed that the doctor had not yet dictated his notes and they could not call for an authorization for the MRI until he had done so. Frustrated, I called my insurance company myself and got the ball rolling. Meanwhile, my primary care doctor had informed me that the results of the bloodwork were all normal except for a Vitamin D deficiency. This is actually one of the latest fads. You can remedy a Vitamin D deficiency by going out in the sun without sunscreen and thereby risking skin cancer or by ingesting a daily supplement of Vitamin D. Since it was mid-December and my peculiar gait problems prevented long walks in the sunlight, I began taking a supplement.

Two days later, I called the neurology office and was told once again that the doctor had not dictated his notes. Two hours after my phone call they called me back with an authorization number, acknowledging that I had initiated the request for authorization myself and the Insurance Company had actually contacted them. More than a week had gone by since my initial neurology appointment.

I speedily made an appointment for an MRI of my brain. I was so thrilled to be doing something that might give me an answer that I nearly dove into the MRI machine. Luckily I am neither claustrophobic nor unable to keep still for a modest period of time because the

MRI tech restrained my head in a wire cage so that I was unable to move my head even a half-inch for the entire forty-five minutes of the test. I felt like Hannibal Lecter but I sailed through the test without difficulty, desperate only to find out what the hell was wrong with me. At the completion of the test I was given a disc of the MRI and told that I would have to wait for a radiologist to read the pictures before I could find out what was officially wrong with my brain. Meanwhile, there would be no unofficial opinions offered as to the cause of my symptoms.

After several days of trying to reach my neurologist by telephone (his office had a voice-mail-only system) my own physician called to see how I was doing and notified me that the brain MRI had come back negative. Which is to say that I had a brain but, contrary to the opinion of some people, it was free of visible disease. Another two days went by before my neurologist phoned me and gave me startling news. My MRI was indeed negative but contrary to my own physician's interpretation of my lab results, my bloodwork had come back positive for Lymes disease.

Chapter 6

<u>Lyme's Merry-go-round</u>

Long Island may not be the epicenter of the tick-borne spirochete infection known as Lyme's Disease but it's close. Several of my friends or their children had contracted Lymes and I often engaged in activities that would place me at risk for a deer tick bite. I loved to hike in the woods, kayak and camp, all of which I had done in the months immediately before my symptoms appeared. In that same time period I had also visited a barn and walked through a grassy field in Northern Connecticut with my daughter who was a Lieutenant in the Governor's Horse Guard. Many of the horses at the barn were known to be positive for Lymes Disease. So the diagnosis not only made sense but it was a relief to finally know what was causing my symptoms and that it could be cured by antibiotics.

When I questioned the fact that my primary care doctor had said that all of my tests were negative both he and the neurologist complained that the lab sheets were confusing to them as printed out from the lab that had performed my tests. So, at first glance, they had perceived the results as negative.

As part of my job I scrutinize the results of a large number of lab tests. I have noted mistakes in interpretation by many nurses over the years of my practice and I make a point of illustrating the possible pitfalls to all new nurses that I train. Perhaps this is one of the reasons that I understood and accepted the possibility of a mistake in the interpretation of my blood tests. Not that it inspired a measure of confidence in me in regard to my doctors. My main concern was to begin treatment as expeditiously as possible so that I could be cured and return to work and normal function. By this time my legs were numb up to my knees and my left arm was becoming weaker by the day. My toes felt stiff and crunchy the way they had felt in the past when they were half frozen inside a pair of ski boots. But the neurologist didn't agree with the idea of immediate treatment and instead insisted that the test be repeated and verified by the University Hospital lab at Stony Brook.

The prospect of waiting longer before getting treatment sent me into a tailspin that was only made worse by well-meaning friends who called daily to ask why I wasn't seeking treatment at my own hospital since they apparently weren't taking very good care of me on the North Shore. But my hospital was an additional thirty minutes travel time and driving was becoming difficult due to the fact that my feet felt like a pair of dead fish.

I went to the Stony Brook lab early the next morning. Christmas had come and gone in a blur and I felt like I was dying. It was now the day before New Years Day and the lab was closing at noon. Another week was wasted while I waited for the results only to find out that they were inconclusive; neither positive nor negative.

By this time I had done quite a bit of research on Lyme's disease, in particular Lymes with central nervous system involvement. If the infection is noticed early, Lymes can be easily treated with a short dose of oral antibiotics. But 80% or less of the time, there is no bulls-eye rash or the patient never sees the rash. And the actual deer tick is so tiny that it can easily go unnoticed. Unfortunately once the disease has proliferated in the central nervous system to the point that it caused symptoms like I was experiencing, the treatment involved probable hospitalization and insertion of a PICC (peripherally inserted central catheter) for long-term intravenous antibiotics. Because of the ability of the Lymes spirochete to become encapsulated and hide from the antibiotics there was a potential that the treatment could last for months if not years. One common thread in the literature was that not only was there a great deal of controversy over long term treatment, probably fueled by the insurance companies who were loath to shell out long term money, but it was important to obtain a "Lymes Literate Doctor". Only a specialist in Lymes would understand that Lyme's was not only known to mimic many other diseases from strokes to MS but that there is really no definitive test for this disease. False negative lab results occur 30-50% of the time. And despite the fact that Lymes is a prevalent and potentially devastating disease, there is relatively little focus on it in the medical profession.

My primary care physician broke the news to me that the neurologist wanted me to undergo more testing. Convinced that there were nasty little spirochetes crawling around inside my brain, I just wanted to start treatment. My needle phobia was totally eclipsed by my desire to feel normal again. I would have held out my arm and let them insert the line without even a local at this point.

It was nearly impossible to reach the neurologist and sometimes you just need a champion. My primary care doctor came to my rescue and intervened. I sat in his waiting room for an hour while *he* tried to reach the neurologist. After an hour he sent me home, promising to call me as soon as he had conversed with the neurologist. He valiantly pushed my case that sending me for yet another blood test and delaying treatment for another two to three weeks was cruel and unusual punishment. But in the end, the neurologist finally called me at home (I can just picture my own doctor telling him, "Fine. You want her to go for another round of tests? Then you call her!") I begged him to put me in the hospital and begin treatment, convinced that I would finally be cured and able to get on with my life. But he still wasn't comfortable treating me for central nervous system Lymes because the insurance company might not cover the cost of the treatment. I argued that we should at least contact the company and find out. He still rigidly refused to do that. He wanted me to go for further testing: a spinal tap. If that came back positive for Lymes, he would consider starting antibiotic treatment.

Chapter 7

Lyme's Round Two: The Spinal Tap

Nearly a week went by before I could arrange for the guided needle spinal tap. This is a test that I would not recommend to anybody. I was initially under the impression that the test would be done with, at the very least, some good drugs. I was mistaken. As a Labor and Delivery nurse. I frequently assist with epidural and spinal anesthesia so I had seen the procedure up close and personal. But my patients were pregnant so the welfare of the fetus was a consideration when giving sedation to the mother. Pregnancy was definitely not an issue with me, and other non-pregnant friends who had undergone spinal procedures, such as epidural for pain relief, had reported it as a comfortable procedure during which they were quite sedated by the performing physician.

One of the things that made the test even more onerous to me was the fact that my research had revealed that *Lyme antibodies show up in Cerebral Spinal Fluid less than 13% of the time in patients who have Lymes meningitis*. In other words I was having a painful test done for no other reason than to appease my neurologist so that he would finally begin to treat me. And there was a good chance, *an 87% chance*, that the results would come back negative even if there were hoards of syphilitic type creepy crawlers nesting in my frontal lobe.

Nearly six weeks of sick time had been burned through by this time and my symptoms were still worsening. Perhaps if I had been able to spend at least a small part of that ugly winter weather under a palm tree while clutching a drink with one if those little paper umbrellas it would have been more palatable. But eating up time off from work in the gloomy months of December and January while you are barely able to walk and certainly unable to ski is hideous. Added to that was a constant barrage of phone calls from my friends at work hounding me for nonexistent test results or to dump my obviously incompetent neurologist and travel down to the South Shore for treatment. I know that they all meant well; I'm blessed with unbelievably caring friends. But not really knowing what was wrong with my body was driving me insane and fielding their phone calls was now only adding to my frustration because I had no answers to give them.

The only good thing about the spinal tap was that my daughter came down from Connecticut to hang out with me. She dropped me off at the entrance to the Emergency Room where patients who had outpatient procedures or surgeries were admitted and drove off to park the car while I waited to be called in to a cubicle. After the usual admission procedure that included drawing blood (I was slowly beginning to deal with my needle phobia due to a greater wish to have my condition diagnosed and cured!) a young man appeared with a wheelchair. He said he was there to take me for my X-ray. I asked if my daughter could come and should we bring our things with us?

"Oh you don't need to- we'll be coming right back after the X-ray."

"So you're not bringing me for the spinal tap now?" I asked, not sure of the procedure for an outpatient spinal tap and surmising that perhaps a chest X-ray was necessary since I was over forty years old. "Sure we don't need to bring the stretcher for recovery and the return trip? "

He glanced down at the slip of paper in his hand and replied, "Nope. Just an X-ray."

What did I know?

There ensued a long and winding wheelchair trip to Radiology. We arrived only to find out that I was indeed there for the spinal tap and did indeed need my stretcher. Back to the Emergency Room by wheelchair, get assigned a locker to store my things and then transfer back to my stretcher before renegotiating the maze of hallways back to the Radiology Department. A real confidence building way to start the morning.

Another young gentleman awaiting my arrival assisted me onto the procedure table and began to position me for the spinal tap. "I don't have an IV yet." I pointed out.

"Oh you won't need an IV." He replied.

In the Delivery Room we always preload patients with an enormous amount of IV fluid prior to an epidural to prevent a blood pressure drop from the anesthesia. I wasn't getting anesthesia, but I was still surprised that I didn't need an IV. I was also quite alarmed. "So where do you put the drugs in?"

"Drugs?" he appeared puzzled.

"Isn't this done with conscious sedation?" I asked, referring to the intravenous infusion of a combination of drugs that would prevent me from experiencing or caring about the pain of the procedure and make my morning pleasant in the bargain.

"I don't think you're going to need drugs."

"You've got another think coming," replied my inner voice. Or maybe this time it was my real voice that spoke to the young man who wasn't quite as handsome as when I first met him a few minutes ago.

The Interventional Radiologist entered the room, introduced himself and reinforced the glorious news that I would be awake for the procedure, which might take a very long time depending on how long it took to drain my spinal fluid for the tests. Then he handed me a clipboard with a consent that I grudgingly signed.

Positioned face down on the table for the spinal tap I was able to fantasize that I was there for an aromatherapy massage until I felt the burning pain of the local anesthetic enter the skin on my lower back followed by the dull piercing nip of the needle. Then suddenly a shooting pain down my right leg that initiated some championship silent cursing at my neurologist who was putting me through this totally ridiculous and unnecessary test. Cursing only by my inner voice, of course, but I did notify the radiologist that my right leg had become decidedly uncomfortable.

"Sorry," said the radiologist, adjusting the needle in order to relieve the unpleasant sensation.

For some reason it took a long time to drain enough fluid for all of the tests. Fifty minutes to be exact including the episode when the fluid stopped draining altogether and the radiologist had to return and fiddle with the needle, initiating another shooting pain from my right buttock that traveled down the back of my right leg.

The pain in my butt lasted to a lesser extent for more than a week. It took more than a week to receive the test results. They were inconclusive as expected. Keanu Reeves was still uncomfortable about beginning a course of antibiotics for Lyme's disease. Sitting in his office I observed his vexation that mirrored my own as he studied my chart. Frustrated and angry, I finally decided it was time to fire my neurologist.

Chapter 8

Time For a Change

Americans believe that they have the most advanced health care system in the world. The truth is, Americans spend a higher amount of their gross domestic product on health services than any other country in the world. But the system doesn't deliver the quality health care that the cost should warrant. A wealthy area might have an abundance of MRI machines but because there is no central planning, if you live in the boondocks or in a poor area you might have to travel to another state to get an MRI. That's if your insurance plan authorizes the test that your doctor has ordered. Our infant mortality rate as compared to other industrialized nations has hovered around 12th place for decades. The number of hospital beds has declined even as the population has expanded and there is a serious worldwide nursing shortage. If you break an arm and go to an Emergency room they will apply a soft cast that is little more than a splint and tell you to make an appointment with an Orthopedist. It may be weeks before you can get an appointment by which time the bone has healed incorrectly. Even in a Trauma Center, a Radiologist is unlikely to view your X-Rays on the spot. It's not uncommon to receive a telephone call several days after an Emergency Room visit only to be told that the arm or leg that you were told was sprained is, in fact, broken and needs to be set.

Another blight on the face of our healthcare system is the Old Boys Club atmosphere that has been fostered for centuries. Doctors close ranks tighter than the Men in Blue and will rarely admit publicly to any deficiencies in one of their peers. They can be extremely edgy about "stealing" patients from their colleagues. But I wasn't just looking for a second opinion; I had basically fired my doctor.

Well aware of the shortcomings of our healthcare system, I knew that obtaining a timely appointment with another neurologist would have been impossible without pulling some strings. Lucky for me, an old friend, an Emergency Physician who works at Stony Brook University Hospital, pulled the strings for me. He happened to be friends with the head of the Neurology department and was able to secure an appointment for me within a week. Since I wasn't able to work or do much more than sit on the couch and watch TV, something I rarely did prior to my illness, my calendar was entirely free.

Deciding to keep my last scheduled appointment with Keanu Reeves, I came armed with the fax number for the new doctor so that my records could be expeditiously faxed over. The visit began with the usual neurological exam that revealed the continued lack of a patellar (knee jerk) reflex in my right leg along with a hyperactive response in the left leg.

"That's baffling," said Neurologist Number One.

"Jesus Christ," replied my inner voice. This was getting old.

Retiring to his office after the physical exam I informed him that I was going to see another neurologist and wanted all of my records faxed over. As I handed him a card with her office fax number he waved his hand, "Not necessary! I have her number. She trained me over at Stony Brook. "

"No really...take it please. I'm seeing her a week from today and want to be sure that she has received all of my records and tests."

Reluctantly he took the card and then opened my chart, which was sitting on the desk in front of him. On top of the pile of papers was a five-page medical history questionnaire that I had filled out on my first visit to his office over seven weeks ago. As he scanned the first page his eyes widened when they lit upon my long-term history of cervical arthritis.

"I'd like you to go for a cervical spine MRI," he suggested. "What's your insurance again?"

"I need authorization and it took a long time to get it for the Brain MRI. Because your office girl said that the notes hadn't been dictated by you and they couldn't apply for authorization until it was."

"Okay," he seemed to let the veiled accusation slide right off. "I'll put in for it today so you can have it done before your appointment next week. "Meanwhile I think you should be using a cane."

"A cane?" I thought. That's for old people!

"Well just for balance, you know."

No way in hell was I getting a cane!

Again I went through the routine of calling his office for five days in a row in an attempt to obtain authorization for the MRI only to be told that he had not yet dictated my chart so they could not apply for authorization. On the fifth day I finally received authorization and immediately went for a cervical MRI. Luckily they give you an actual disc with the pictures before you leave since a radiologist doesn't review and write an interpretation of the MRI immediately. Armed with the disc I visited my new neurologist two days later.

Chapter 9

Finally a Diagnosis

Three telephone calls should have been sufficient to ensure that my records would be faxed over to my new neurologist. In a perfect world. After an exhaustive neurological exam my new doctor glanced at the few pages that had been faxed from my prior doctors office.

"They faxed my records, right?" I inquired. "I had a lot of tests and bloodwork done in the last two months. And I specifically asked to have the results of my MRIs sent over."

"There's not much here- just these two pages," the Chief of Neurology at Stony Brook rather testily replied before she picked up a telephone and called the front desk to request another telephone call to Keanu Reeves.

"I did bring the disc from my most recent MRI," I suggested hopefully.

"Good. Come next door and I'll take a look at it in the computer."

A doctor who was actually going to look at and interpret the MRI disc herself? Sweet! In fact, her entire affect, brisk, professional and confident was reassuring; miles above the relaxed Keanu Reeves dress and persona of my first neurologist. I felt like I might actually be on the verge of receiving a real diagnosis! I was correct. As she viewed the film on disc from the MRI, a secretary entered bearing a faxed copy of my Cervical MRI that this doctor ignored, at least for the moment.

Gesturing me over to the computer screen, she pointed to the severely scalloped column of my neck. "Did you have a recent injury?" she inquired.

"No."

"You have very severe arthritis as well as several herniated discs. And do you see this area here?" she pointed to a white tube like structure within my spinal cord. "You have a lesion on your spinal cord. That's what is causing your symptoms."

"A lesion?" My knees suddenly felt close to collapse and I grabbed the edge of the counter for support. I took a deep breath. "Is it cancer?"

"No. Cancer is almost always outside the spinal column. This is at the level of your spine that has the worst disease. I think that is what has caused the lesion. The spinal canal has become so narrow that your spinal cord is compressed. And compression on your cord may have caused a vascular injury."

At this point she picked up and read the radiology interpretation of the MRI that had been faxed over. "No, they're wrong." I can't even pronounce what the radiologist called the lesion and I didn't have to learn because apparently he was wrong anyway.

The doctors' gaze bored into me when she said, "I want you in Stony Brook immediately. I'll arrange for a neurosurgeon to see you as expeditiously as possible. You need decompression immediately if you want to avoid permanent paralysis."

I don't believe she had the slightest comprehension of the thoughts that were suddenly clanging around inside my head. On the one hand, despite the horrifying word *paralysis*, I was thrilled to finally have a diagnosis. She, of course, had no way of knowing that I had desperately been walking around, no, shuffling around for nearly two months while my legs turned into rubber and the burning pain in my left arm threatened to immolate me. Still, as I mentioned earlier, I have been a "scalpophobe" since Nursing School, managing to avoid surgery and hospitalizations except for a solitary incident when my horse tripped and I broke my wrist into a thousand pieces (a very painful memory indeed). If not for the obvious deformity and boneless lack of support for my hand without a working wrist, I probably would have avoided surgery in that instance too. An unabashed coward to the bone, I dodged needles like the plague; it generally took at least two colleagues to accompany my pathetic whining self down to Employee Health for my yearly PPD test, a tiny prick given just below the skin that tests for tuberculosis. And now she was talking neuro-s-word. Cutting into my spine!

Another thought that was nearly as problematic was the fact that I didn't think I had medical coverage for Stony Brook hospital. And you don't want to have major surgery without medical coverage. Prior to my divorce a few months back it wasn't a problem since I had additional medical coverage under my husband's health plan. But now I was limited to my own health plan and, despite the fact that my employers and I contributed thousands of dollars a year to supply me with coverage, I was pretty sure that my choice of hospitals might be limited to the hospitals within Catholic Health Services (CHS). Once a year I was able to select my health care plan from my employer. I had always chosen the medium-priced plan that offered coverage for nearly all physicians as well as coverage for any hospital in the CHS. The most expensive plan seemed to offer less coverage. With that plan you could go to *any* hospital but it would actually cost more to be hospitalized than if you had the medium priced plan and went to a hospital in the network. The CHS network included St. Francis Hospital, one of the most prestigious heart hospitals in the region, my own institution (Good Samaritan Hospital Medical Center) and a third hospital, St. Charles, that was a few miles away from where I lived. Figuring that the most probable reason for me to need hospitalization was cancer or a heart attack (can you tell that I'm a gambler?) I thought that I had all my bases covered. Good Sam had great oncologists and St. Francis was the best choice for the ticker. In a crunch, St.

Charles could handle bumps, sprains or broken bones. Trouble was, St. Charles was a relatively small community hospital that specialized in Rehabilitation and it looked like I now needed what only a University Hospital could offer; the best neurosurgeons in the area. Chances were that they didn't do neurosurgery at St. Charles. Nevertheless, I gave it the good old college try, "Could I go to St. Charles for the surgery?"

She shot me a look that said, "Are you daft girl?" (I had the feeling that she too had an inner voice) but what she actually offered in a rather condescending tone was, "*I* don't go to St. Charles but perhaps your doctor knows somebody…"

Then she picked up the phone and dialed my doctor. Getting him on the line rather quickly, I was shocked to hear how she phrased my response to the situation. After explaining my diagnosis to him, she said, "The patient is refusing to go to the hospital."

Now that is definitely *not* what I said (even though I must admit that the scalpophobe part of me was on the verge…) but she repeated the phrase at least three times before I was summarily ushered out of her office in a mingled state of confusion and panic. She now wore a look on her face that said I was wasting her time.

I don't recall how I made it home. Alone in the comfort and quiet of my own living room I was able to assess the situation more clearly. Realizing that this was probably one of the most momentous decisions I would ever make in my life, I sat unmoving for nearly an hour, wishing that there was someone I could call for advice. My Mom, my closest friend and advisor, was out of reach since she had died seven years ago. Ditto my ex-husband who would have been the first person I would have turned to in the past. No. This decision was going to have to be made by me and me alone. I began to wonder if I was wrong about not having coverage at Stony Brook hospital. The idea of having spinal surgery at St. Charles began to seem as ludicrous to me as the look on my doctors' face had portended. And the whole time that I sat wondering what the hell I was going to do I could hear her voice tripping through my head like a litany. "The patient is refusing to go to the hospital. The patient is refusing to go to the hospital. The patient…" My legs barely worked. It felt like I was wearing heavy cold boots up to my knees. My fingers were so stiff and cramped that it was difficult to type and my left arm was getting weaker by the day. Tingling rivers of burning pain licked at my left upper arm. Paralysis. Paralysis.

I reached for the phone.

Chapter 10

Stony Brook

Verifying that I was indeed still covered for treatment at Stony Brook was established with a simple phone call but reaching the neurologist to apprise her of my change of heart was a little more difficult. A busy woman, she was already gone from the office and not expected back until the following week. Meanwhile, my spine was collapsing and all I could see when I closed my eyes was the three centimeter tube-like lesion inside my spinal cord that was causing my body to malfunction. Panic gripped my chest with a sudden urgency and I began to tremble. Now that I had come face to face with the culprit who was sabotaging my body my worries took on a more concrete form. One question that I had been asked repeatedly in the past two months was an inquiry into the state of my bowel and bladder function. Jesus Christ, I thought. Do not- pleeeeeaaaase- do NOT make me incontinent on top of all the other symptoms. Picturing waste products running unchecked down my legs or facing the possibility of spending the rest of my life with an indwelling foley catheter, I was suddenly in a hurry to get fixed, even if it meant being on the other side of the siderail.

After repeated attempts spurred on with increasing desperation, I was finally able to reach the neurologists' secretary and pass on a message that I had been mistaken about lacking coverage at Stony Brook and I was willing to come in immediately for butchery. Actually I believe that my real voice used the word *surgery*. Then I sat back to wait for her reply. I couldn't eat or sleep or read or watch TV. I was afraid to go to the bathroom; what if she called? Every minute seemed like an hour. Sometime in the wee hours I drifted off to sleep on top of my comforter.

She finally responded the following day with instructions and the news that my admission had been arranged. With mixed feelings of joy and doom, I presented myself to the Emergency Room at Stony Brook University Hospital where our mutual friend had secured a bed for me since there were no beds on the main units of the hospital, hard to believe since Stony Brook University Hospital as seen from the outside looks like it could house an entire city.

The obvious result of refusing treatment as well as the glaring deficits in function that I was experiencing allowed me to readily offer my arms in sacrifice to the Gods of Intravenous Fluids and Bloodtests. It was an immeasurable comfort to have my daughter once again by my side as I waited for test results and underwent further testing, including a cervical CAT Scan and an additional MRI, this time with contrast dye. Luckily I am not claustrophobic; my solitary fear is confined to the piercing of my skin by sharp objects such as scalpels, needles and bee stings. It's amazing that I ever got my ears pierced. Many people, including at least one close friend, are terrified of being restrained inside the close confines of a CAT Scan or MRI machine but I was thankfully able to close my eyes and ignore the pounding and buzzing with ease.

Late in the evening a Neurosurgical PA (Physicians Assistant) approached me to lay out the plan of action. Apparently operating near the spinal cord when the nerves are already inflamed is not a great idea so I would be put on a regimen of high dose intravenous steroids for several days before the surgery was performed. Hopefully the surgery would relieve the pressure on my spinal cord by stabilizing the vertebrae and my symptoms would abate. It was the method of surgery that grabbed my attention and threatened to disrupt my self-control. They planned to operate on my spine by cutting my throat.

My hands flew protectively to my neck at the thought and I'm not sure that I was able to absorb anything else that the PA said to me after that point. I'm pretty sure that I made him repeat the description of what he called an Anterior Fusion more than once.

Touted as a much less invasive surgery than a posterior fusion, where the surgeons enter from the back (where the spinal column is, Hello!) an anterior fusion is supposed to be less painful and less invasive. But it sounded absolutely barbaric. Who was the first person to think of doing the procedure that way? And who was the first patient who said, "Okay. Sure. You need to get to my spine. Yeah, you can cut my throat…" Like Jack the f-ing Ripper. I couldn't close my eyes without visualizing a scalpel being dragged across my throat, creating a long, blood-filled smile above my chest.

I suddenly wished that I had never assisted in surgery or seen it up close and personal. At the same time I was deliriously happy that I had never scrubbed on this particular type of surgery. Well, maybe not deliriously happy. It's kind of hard to be deliriously happy about anything when you're about to have your throat cut. More like seriously grateful. Still, for the next several hours, most of the thoughts that pounded through my brain had to do with the hideous prospect of a scalpel cutting my throat and retractors moving aside the soft (and not-so-soft) tissue until the anterior surface of the vertebrae was exposed. Then the buzz of the power tool as the screws were driven into my arthritic bones. What if he slipped and cut my vocal cords or nicked a carotid. How was I possibly going to survive the next three days while a continuous reel of gory, bloody visuals marched through my brain? Minutes ticked by like hours that stretched into years in my featureless, windowless corner of the Emergency Room. More than once I considered getting up and running for the door. It was a scalpelphobes' worst nightmare.

In the end it turned out that I wouldn't have to wait three days after all. In the wee hours of the night, long after my daughter had left, I heard muted voices followed by footsteps approaching from the darkened corridor. The Neurosurgical PA had returned. His kind eyes and gentle voice were a balm to my shattered nerves and his news stole the breath from my lungs. The neurosurgeon had finally come in and reviewed my latest films. My spine was too unstable and he didn't want to wait three days for the steroids to work after all. For two months I had suffered an agony of impatience while trying to find out what was wrong with me, but now my world, my future was speeding out of control. He would operate first thing in the morning.

Chapter 11

Getting My Throat Cut

As the news sank in, I actually heaved a great sigh of relief. I wouldn't have to wait several days after all while my courage seeped away in a stream of horrible images of sliced throats and bloodied bones. By this time tomorrow night the ordeal would all be over.

I wasn't afraid of death. That had never been a fear of mine. In fact, I was convinced that dying under anesthesia would be a rather nice way to go. It was just the idea of the type of surgery, taking a blade and slicing my throat open that scared me. It reminded me of a guillotine except for the fact that my surgery would take a lot longer than the French method of throat-slicing. As a nurse I had seen stab wounds and gunshot wounds before as well as nearly every possible type of abdominal, chest and limb surgery. But the worst sights, at least for me, had always been the neck surgeries.

Back in the early 1970's when I was working at The Roosevelt Hospital on Manhattans' west side, I had cared for many patients with cancer of the throat, larynx, tongue or neck and the surgery done on them was often creatively horrific. One older gentleman who had been a friend of mine before the surgery had a full thickness skin graft harvested from his forehead to cover his neck, leaving him with a Frankenstein-like visage. He was always well dressed and nearly always sported an old-fashioned fedora. The hat would now become a necessity if he wasn't in the mood for scaring little children on the subway. Sometimes a skin flap would be left partially attached until it was needed to cover the gaping hole that would be left when the cancer was removed. The surgery was in fact so grotesque that I had always been convinced that I would never report or admit to a tumor in my throat or neck since I would never let them do that to me. I knew on a conscious level that I wasn't having cancer surgery and that this didn't even compare to my memories. But the idea of having my throat cut...

I must have finally dozed off after sending text messages to my daughter and son that the surgery had been moved up. Over the course of the next two months texting would become a staple of my nocturnal activities since I was often awake in the wee hours and needed to communicate but did not wish to wake up my family and friends. I didn't want to wake my children if they had fallen asleep but was afraid that my daughter would be upset if she showed up in my room in the morning and I was missing with no explanation. An institution as large as Stony Brook can be impersonal and information as to my whereabouts might not have been easily forthcoming.

Prior to the surgery I was moved up from the Emergency Room to the Neurology unit where my films were visible on a portable television set in the hallway. I remember feeling somewhat important that my spine was of such interest to the gaggle of medical students and residents who were staring at the screen. They eyed me solemnly as I was wheeled past them before returning their attention to the monitor that held the image of my spine. Instead of a nice straight tube, the canal inside my vertebrae where my spinal cord resided looked like a scalloped tunnel. Quite decorative, actually. And toward the left side of my spinal cord was the sinister white opacity of the tube-like lesion that was causing my symptoms.

Just before I drifted off to sleep for the night I received a text message answer from my son. At that time he was employed as a Paramedic in Boston, but he had received his original Paramedic training at Stony Brook. His dry sense of humor prevented an ordinary response to the news of my impending surgery. No "Good luck Mom" or "Hope the operation goes well" from him. He knew that a little levity was what I desperately needed to keep me from jumping ship at the last moment. His text said simply, "Don't let a Paramedic student intubate you."

My entry into the operating area was actually anticlimactic. My surgeons and two anesthesiologists met me at the door. I commented on how special I felt having two anesthesiologists but didn't really want to know why. I was meeting my surgeon for the first time and was glad to note that he was quite attractive. These things are important. I wouldn't want an ugly man cutting my throat. In fact he looked something like Sean Connery but lacked a Scottish accent. Pity. As I signed the written consent that he held out to me one of the anesthesiologists injected something into a port in my IV tube and I slid off into the Twilight Zone.

I awoke in the Recovery Room numb from the waist down. More than the type of numb you feel under a local anesthetic like a dentist gives you; I couldn't feel anything. Was I paralyzed? I gingerly drew the sheet up to expose my feet and discovered the tubing of a foley catheter snaking down off the side of the stretcher. For the uninitiated, a foley is a long, soft rubber tube with a hole toward one end that gets inserted into the urinary bladder via the urethra. The other end of the tube is connected to a bag that the urine drains into. The end that is actually in the bladder has a balloon that can be remotely inflated by injecting 10cc of sterile water into the far end with a syringe. The balloon keeps the foley seated inside the neck of the bladder unless an undue amount of force is placed upon the catheter. I have seen them accidently ripped out more than once, a rather traumatic event that results in a significant bit of roadburn in the urethra. And yes, foley catheters are unisex and, although the insertion method varies slightly, the same exact product is used for both males and females. The reaction by patients to foley catheters has been so varied in my experience that I did not know what to expect. Most patients have little or no complaints but many people complain of discomfort every time the catheter is moved in the slightest. In any event, I decided that perhaps my current state of numbness was a good thing.

Experimenting further, I waved my feet back and forth and wiggled my toes. Okay, I might be numb but my stuff still worked. So maybe everything was going to be okay. Apparently I wasn't paralyzed. There wasn't even much pain in my throat. Only a kind of stiffness in my neck. The worst soreness was a spasm in my right trapezius, the muscle between my neck and shoulder that stretches down toward the spine. I had suffered from pain in that area for years, although not as strong as I was feeling at the time. Reassured, I fell back to sleep.

I didn't wake up again until I was in my room back on the Neurology unit. Despite my vigorous protests, they had made me remove my panties prior to leaving for the operating room even though the surgery wasn't remotely connected to that section of my anatomy. (I realize now that they needed access to insert the foley catheter.) I lifted the sheet again and, yes; the foley was still there. I also noted that a pair of Sequential TEDs were wrapped around my legs.

TEDs are disposable Velcro-fastened leggings that are applied to the lower extremities and connected by tubing to a machine that intermittently pumps air into the leggings. The resulting action is like a massage that purportedly assists in the movement of blood through your veins. This in turn will hopefully prevent the formation of blood clots. Once a clot forms, the greatest danger is that it will travel up to the heart and from there into the lungs, an event that is often fatal. Prior to the practice of making people ambulate as soon as possible after surgery, a traveling clot or embolism was not an uncommon cause of postoperative death. Some people have a higher risk of developing blood clots than others. Pregnant women are particularly prone to this ominous complication, as are people with certain pre-existing diseases. Anyone with a prior history of a blood clot, heart attack or stroke has a greater risk. Also at risk is anyone who smokes or has a sedentary lifestyle. I had suffered from a blood clot in my right calf shortly after my daughter was born. And while I had tossed the cancer sticks, I had spent the better part of the last two months glued to my couch because of the weakness in my legs. I was also going to be on strict bedrest until the next day. So I was definitely a candidate for TEDs until I could ambulate.

The thing about TEDs is that without the machine to inflate them, they are basically a useless pair of leg warmers. There was no inflation unit at the end of my bed.

Presently a nurse entered my room and blessedly offered treatment for my pain, which had become more than annoying as the anesthesia drugs wore off. When I requested an inflation machine for my TEDs she was unable to comply, however, since there were none available. This I can relate to. We frequently run out of TED machines in my own hospital. In fact, equipment failure and hospital overcrowding coupled with budgetary constraints often leads to a shortage of equipment. And the missing equipment is often much more important than Sequential TEDs. Pumps malfunction, people call in sick and sometimes there are manufacturer backorders. Because of an imperfect world, we cannot always deliver the highest quality of care to our patients and I was willing to overlook the absence of a TEDs machine as long as my nurse kept the Dilaudid coming.

Personable and pleasant, she began to tell me about the career change that had led her to the nursing profession. There is currently a nursing shortage far beyond the cyclical shortages that periodically plague many professions. While men do enter the profession, women have traditionally populated nursing. Despite the sexual revolution, women and female professions still command a lower salary than those that tend to employ men. And with so many options now open to women, the idea of shouldering huge responsibilities over long shifts that encompass weekends, night shifts and holidays for relatively low pay may seem less attractive. Not to mention the exposure to gore and bodily fluids that, in addition to being unattractive and odoriferous, carry deadly diseases. These things have never bothered me since, corny as it may sound, I have always felt a calling for the profession and consider nursing more a statement of what I am than what I do for a living. That isn't always the case for a large number of people entering the profession today. The average nurse is close to my age (over 50 and that's all I'm going to say for now.) We are all about to retire in a decade or so if the physical requirements of the job, including standing on our feet for hours at a time, lifting patients and performing other tasks lacking in ergonometric benefits don't force an early retirement upon us.

The nursing shortage is worldwide and not limited to industrialized nations. In fact, many industrialized nations like the U.S. have taken to robbing poorer nations of their nurses by enticing them with promises of housing, assistance in procuring the credentials to practice here and a higher salary than they had ever imagined. This is a cruel practice in more ways than one. Less prosperous nations often invest an inordinate amount of their resources into training nurses only to have them scooped up by a more affluent nation. Because of low salaries in the mother country, the offerings from places like the United States must seem like a dream come true and, indeed, if one lives frugally it might even be possible to subsist here while sending a little dough home for the family. My own hospital has engaged in the recruiting of foreign nurses with limited success. Their language skills are often found wanting, a circumstance that could lead to a sometimes dangerous situation as well as prevent them from passing the Nursing Boards. The practice of nursing, especially regarding the focus of practice, differs widely in many less fortunate countries. In the United States, for instance, it has been documented by extensive research that the alleviation of pain is of paramount importance in the healing process. The pain level has, in fact, been called the "fifth vital sign", accompanying the measurement of blood pressure, temperature, pulse and respirations. Several "pain scales" have been invented to more accurately measure pain and patients are constantly quizzed on their pain level. In contrast is a story I once heard from a nurse who trained in Poland. She sited the use of pain relief medication in her native country as being far different from our own. When she was practicing there, a prescription for pain relief medication would be written for a patient undergoing surgery. Your family would have to go to a pharmacy, purchase the medication and bring it to the hospital where a nurse would inject it. If you were short on funds, well, here's a piece of leather you can bite on...

One argument against the procurement of foreign nurses put forth by nurses here in the United States is that the recruitment money spent to lure nurses here from Africa, the Philippines or India could have been better spent raising the salaries of American nurses and even offering us health care benefits at retirement. When I retire from a lifetime spent caring for the sick and injured I will have no health insurance. That may not matter since there won't be anyone left in the nursing field to take care of me and studies have shown that the most important element in recovery lies in the attendance of a Registered Nurse.

In an extreme effort to stave off the nursing shortage, many Universities have developed programs that lure people from other professions. These programs often have a seriously limited amount of training in nursing skills. If you have a few prerequisites in science you might become an RN in as little as one year. As long as you can pass the boards, you are licensed as a Registered Nurse. When I took my Nursing boards I sat in an old armory in Jamaica, Queens for two grueling days while each aspect of nursing, including Pediatrics, Medicine, Surgery, Obstetrics, and Psychiatry were rigorously tested. Failing one aspect meant you failed the whole thing. Period. I have heard from new nurses that the exam is now given by computer and the computer shuts off when you have answered a sufficient amount of questions to be deemed proficient as a nurse. This is often after as few as eighty questions. Most nursing programs today offer almost no hands-on clinical experience. A graduate nurse may have never given an injection, let alone started an IV, drawn blood, inserted a foley catheter, assisted in surgery or even changed a dressing. They may have *observed* these procedures. But the lion's share of training in the Nursing Profession today revolves around the nursing process, theory and problem solving, leaving little room for actually laying hands on a suffering human being. (Sorry to cause a lack of faith in the profession but bottom line: the person pricking you might be doing it for the first time even if her nametag says "RN".)

My nurse on the day after surgery happened to be another hybrid nurse that had migrated to nursing from another profession outside the healthcare field. She boasted that she had just started working as an RN a short while ago after completing a one-year program. I was content with this information as long as adequate pain medication was forthcoming. I had been confronted with substandard nursing care many times before while navigating through numerous parental hospitalizations and I was confident that I could avert any dire catastrophe. The anesthesia had was worn off for the most part and I was once again cognizant of my surroundings.

On strict bedrest for the first twenty-four hours after surgery, I was now going to be allowed out of bed. My newly graduated nurse removed my foley catheter and advised me that I was on the clock. This is a commonly used threat: Pee within the next four hours *or else* the tube gets reinserted. (My Mom used to use the *or else* technique with me. It's actually a rather effective tool.) I still had an IV dripping fluids into my veins; the lifeline through which pain medications were injected. I was also receiving steroids, which may have been to blame for the frequent infiltration of my IV sites, necessitating additional needles being poked into me. Hopefully the fluids would assist my bladder in achieving the pee-within-four-hours goal. Either that or I would have to lie in order to avert a reinsertion of the foley catheter. Sure I peed. Fountains. I was a regular Niagara Falls in there.

In the end there was no need for prevarication. As the urge came on, I gingerly sat up on the side of the bed and prepared to stand. I didn't want to take a header and chance dislocating my new hardware by falling if I became dizzy. Before standing up I removed the TEDs from my lower legs since there was no machine to inflate them. I would no longer need them anyway, since I was no longer on bedrest. Passing the garbage on the way to the bathroom, I tossed the disposable TEDs into the can.

Shortly after my trip to the bathroom my nurse returned to inquire about my success in the bathroom and to inject pain relief into my vein. I was enjoying the respite from spasms in my upper back after the injection and fading into the sweet arms of Morpheus when she interrupted my bliss with a horrified shriek. Staring in dismay at the garbage can, she lifted the discarded TEDs from the trash and turned a rabid accusing eye upon me.

"You can't throw these out!" she waved the offending items at me, her eyebrows arched in disbelief that I would perpetrate such a crime.

"But they're disposable." I countered. Ha. She wasn't going to make me feel needless guilt. "And there wasn't a machine to hook them up to anyway. I asked for one yesterday and the nurse said that you were out of machines. Besides, I'm not on bedrest anymore so I don't need them."

Her response was a wide-eyed glare as she slammed them down onto my nightstand. On top of my toothbrush and toiletries. The TEDs that she had just removed *from the garbage*. The icky, gross MRSA infested hospital garbage can. Now sitting atop *my* toothbrush. "You still can't just throw them out." She bit out through tightly clenched teeth.

And before either my inner or my outer voice could ask "Why the fuck not?" she preempted my inquiry. "You have a Doctor's order for them!" she screamed before stalking angrily from the room.

Chapter 12

Relapse

Surviving a life crisis is often dependent upon the people around you. I had a much larger support system than I realized. My daughter was a rock and I leaned on her full force while my son kept me smiling with his offbeat sense of humor that I adore. Even his girlfriend came to the rescue when I desperately needed help washing my hair and my arms were too weak. My cousin who had lived only blocks away from me when I was growing up but now lived at the opposite end of Long Island became a frequent visitor and later saved me from the horrible fate of residing in a Nursing Home. Several friends from work made it their business to check up on me both before I was operated on and after I was discharged home. Sometimes I didn't want to answer the telephone but was forced to when a voice floated out of the answering machine, "Answer the phone Donna. Don't MAKE me send an ambulance..."

Jubilant at being home again, I succumbed to the watery daylight of February by sleeping on the couch in between HBO movies. I had never been a television enthusiast, preferring books by far. But my concentration was fleeting and I had difficulty reading more than a page at a time. My left arm was still weak and my legs were shaky but sensation was returning and they no longer felt like cold dead fish attached to my knees. At least my right arm was fully functional although my fingers still felt spastic if I tried to type. My left arm worked fine for petting my cat, who had become increasingly more affectionate after being left alone for so many days. It was just good to be home from the hospital. The only thing I missed was the food. Seriously. The food at Stony Brook University Hospital is better than many restaurants in New York. The cheesecake (with a raspberry melba sauce drizzled on top) was certainly among the best I had ever tasted and was delivered directly to my bed by a suited waiter a short time after placing my order via telephone. That's right. No generic tray service that might arrive when you are sleeping or in Radiology having a test. You receive a menu when you are admitted and place your order by telephone when you get hungry.

Later on I joked that it was the food that brought me back to Stony Brook. I just couldn't get on without the cheesecake. But it was actually my right arm. Two days after being discharged from the hospital I woke up unable to lift my right arm. My mind is still somewhat foggy about what transpired between the time that I discovered my new disability and my arrival at the Emergency Room. Somehow I managed to dress myself before phoning a friend who lived a few miles away and asking for a lift to the hospital. Her husband ran the Paramedic program at the hospital and I had known them both for a long time although I saw them infrequently. For years I had taught several classes in Obstetrics, Gynecology and Trauma in Pregnancy in the Paramedic program each January but I had been unable to teach this year due to my illness. All of my other friends lived at least a half hour away and although I had not seen Karen in ages, she was the first person that I thought of to call. Luckily she was at home and in her generous fashion dropped everything to drive me to the hospital. Her husband Paul met us in the crowded Emergency Room entrance and I was quickly ushered inside and into a bed. They stayed with me for hours until I finally insisted that they go home to their family, assuring them that I would be fine.

It was decided after an hour or so that I needed an MRI with contrast in order to determine what had caused the sudden deterioration in my condition. I knew by now through prior experience that while a CAT Scan could be done in only a few minutes, an MRI with contrast was at least a forty-five minute ordeal. I still wasn't claustrophobic but I knew that I would not be able to remain supine without a neck pillow for that length of time. Furthermore, in my haste to return to the hospital I had neglected to ingest a pain pill and my neck was now literally killing me. In true hospital fashion my request for pain relief was trumped by the Radiology schedule that now had an opening and I was whisked off for an MRI sans medication despite my protests.

Arriving at my destination I gamely attempted to assume the position but was unable to lower my head into the cradle. "Can't I have a pillow?"

The tech was sympathetic but adamant. My head would have to go into the cradle and then be locked into place with a Hannibal Lecter-type cage for the duration of the test. I tried putting my head in that position but the pain had now reached about 8 on a scale of 10 and my eyes were tearing up. "I'm sorry. Can't do it." I apologized.

Back to the Emergency Room and hopefully some relief for my screaming neck. My room had been given away in my absence, perhaps to punish me for being unable to endure the MRI without pain medication, so my stretcher was placed in a hallway. I was able to see the nurses walking by in random states of confusion mixed with importance while hoping that one of them was going to bring me drugs. They avoided eye contact and scurried past, unable or unwilling to help me. My neck was on fire and sweat began to break out on my forehead and upper lip. As time passed the pain became unbearable and despite my attempts at self-hypnosis, a technique I had studied in college, it overwhelmed my senses and I began to experience a crushing chest pain. Having practiced medicine for more than three decades, I knew that crushing chest pain was not a good thing. I also knew that divulging its presence was probably the one thing that would garner attention and possibly even allow me to score some Dilaudid or Morphine.

There is some wretched remnant of my upbringing that commands me to be polite, even in extreme circumstances. Over the years I have witnessed many scenes and tantrums as patients and their families complained loudly about their treatment or demanded to speak to a Nursing Supervisor or even a Hospital Administrator. Despite the fact that these tactics do, in fact, often bring results along with a less than friendly regard by the nursing staff, I have never been able to employ them. Just as I was unable to intervene for my parents, I was unable to stand up for myself until it was nearly too late. In a pathetically mousy voice I flagged down a passing nurse. "Excuse me," I whimpered, finding it difficult now to catch my breath. "I have chest pain."

Magic words. Within minutes I miraculously regained a private room, this time with a cardiac monitor. My blood pressure was 220/120, an amazingly high number that would result in a stroke if it wasn't controlled quickly. The Emergency Room physician, a young Asian, approached my stretcher with a wide smile. "I know you!" he greeted me expectantly. "I was at your party!" Prior to my divorce, when my husband and I lived in Port Jefferson we had hosted some late-night karaoke pool parties that often included members of the Emergency Room staff. But what I needed now wasn't a pleasant reminiscence of a fun-filled night. It seemed a sign of my recent luck that the ER doc had waited until I had an elephant sitting on my chest before he recognized me. "It hurts." I reminded him with a weak smile. Back to Earth, Doc, pleeeeease. "Really bad."

Something in my countenance must have hit home because in a short amount of time I received an Echocardiogram and drugs to control my blood pressure and, blessedly, my pain. (It's not what you know; it's who you know?) After ascertaining that I had not yet had a heart attack and while I was still comfortable enough from the medication, I was wheeled back to Radiology where I was now able to endure a contrast MRI. The rest of the night was spent in an ER holding room. I was to be admitted to a room as soon as one became available. The next morning, apprised of my situation, my ex-husband expedited the process and I was whisked upstairs for more high-dose intravenous steroids. My arm failed to respond to the anti-inflammatory effects of the steroids and my legs had become weaker than they were prior to the first surgery. I was given the bad news by a neurosurgical Physicians Assistant a few days later. It looked like I was going under the knife again.

Chapter 13

<u>Back Under the Knife</u>

Apparently an anterior spinal fusion is a much less invasive surgery than a posterior fusion, despite the nasty idea of having your throat cut with the anterior method. The downside is that, according to my neurosurgeon, a laminectomy (removal of a section of the bone that covers the back of the spinal cord) cannot be performed with the anterior surgery. During the first operation my vertebrae was fused from the level of C4 through C6, a procedure where a metal H-shaped device is screwed into the bones of the spine to hold them in place. During this second surgery they would place a second H-shaped device on the posterior spine, this time at levels C4 through C7. They would also perform four laminectomies and, as I found out several months later, insert bone grafts from cadavers. (Icky!!)

It was the worsening paralysis that had suddenly appeared in my right arm that bought me a return flight to the Operating Room for the more invasive posterior surgery. In a weird sort of déjà vu I met my neurosurgeon outside the door of the OR. Again I signed most of my name to a paper attached to a clipboard that held what I can only suppose was a consent while an anesthesiologist injected the rapture into my IV line. Due to an injury, my original neurosurgeon was unavailable, so his partners were going to operate on me. Considering the short amount of time that I had spent with my neurosurgeon, they could have lied and I never would have known. I would certainly never have been able to pick him out in a line-up. In fact, the janitor could have operated and I wouldn't have caught on. Maybe he did operate the first time and that's why my symptoms got so much worse after the surgery instead of better. Of course the closing stitches had to have been done by a pro because even after such a short amount of time I could hardly make out the scar.

Waking up from the second surgery was similar to the first except that the pain was ratcheted up a few notches. I was either unable or afraid to move my neck very much and since my neck was still attached to my body, I slept in pretty much the same position for several days. That is, on my back, with the head of the bed elevated about 45 degrees. Dilaudid was the only thing that would relieve the burning pain in my neck and upper back. Photos revealed an ugly, bruised and swollen foot-long scar that extended from the shaved lower region of my hairline to the area several inches below the base of my neck.

An additional scar was apparently obtained during the surgery. For the first time that I could remember, the neurosurgeons appeared at my bedside the morning after surgery. Boy did I feel special. Until I realized the reason for their uncomfortable and stilted attendance. Obviously awkward, they proceeded to inform me that a piece of equipment intended to hold my head still for the operation had broken and caused a laceration across my scalp in the back of my head. Apparently the wealth of post-op narcotics had prevented me from noticing the bonus area of shorn locks complete with staples on the upper left posterior of my head. It was surrounded by a halo of hair that was stiff with dried blood.

The brilliance of the neurosurgeon was obvious in his timing; he informed me of the accident directly after seeing that I had received my dose of Dilaudid. I merely smiled in response to the news and most likely would have laughed or made an adorably witty remark (as I am prone to do) if only my lips had been able to coordinate with my tongue. Dilaudid, by the way, is probably the only true reliever of severe pain in our modern pharmacological cornucopia. I am thoroughly convinced that the inventor of this drug should at the very least receive the Nobel Prize. And make more money than the star of the New York Yankees. For several days I would, in true Pavlovian spirit, ring my buzzer in response to the blinding spasms in my neck and upper back. Within moments a syringe-bearing nurse would appear. Even as the magic solution was traveling down the tubing I could actually feel the pain bleeding out of my tissues.

My Affaire de Coeur with Dilaudid probably could have lasted if not for the damn cheesecake. In Stony Brook you have to make a phone call to get fed and I have already stated that the effort is actually worth it. A black vested waiter delivers a tray within minutes that contains whatever culinary delights you have ordered from the menu. But I had to wake up from my drug-induced stupor to eat and that meant learning to deal with the pain. My roommate during this stay had undergone a surgery similar to mine but to her lower spine. She was pleasant and sweet despite being in a great deal of pain. While we were both relative invalids, we attempted to help each other to the best of our ability. One day she was left in her chair, from which she could not arise on her own, and had become extremely uncomfortable as her medication dwindled. Her call bell was out of reach and when I became aware of her situation, I rang for her. There was no response to my buzzer but she was now weeping with pain. The physical therapy department had left a walker near my bed and shown me how to use it earlier, but I wasn't supposed to fly solo. This situation seemed to warrant a breaking of the rules and, being a rebel anyway, I managed to climb out of bed, stand with the walker and make my way to the nursing station for help, all while assuring my friend that help would soon be on the way. As her condition improved, she would sometimes assist me in things I was unable to do because of the weakness of my fingers and arms, like flip the cap on the cans that held my V-8 juice.

The units I occupied were generally peaceful and neat. It's entirely too bad that a similar amount of attention was not paid to patient hygiene. Over the entire course of both hospital stays at University Hospital, I was never bathed or even so much as offered a basin, soap or a washrag. My upper arms were both paralyzed and my legs were extremely weak so while I could manage to feed myself if the tray was placed in front of me, it was nearly impossible to wash or dress. There was a shower in my room but my legs were too shaky to stand for long, even with a walker and the paralysis in my arms prevented me from reaching the shower knobs. I finally begged my son's girlfriend to hose me down while I huddled in a shower chair. It was a mortifying experience but I was desperate to feel clean again.

From the very beginning of my career as a nurse the tenets of personal hygiene have been at the forefront of the ingredients necessary for the preservation of health. At Good Samaritan, where I have worked for over thirty years, a nursing assistant gives all patients who have undergone cesarean section a bed bath after they arrive at the Maternity

Unit. And, unlike me, the patients generally have full use of their arms! Perhaps caring for the physical needs of a patient is a lost art in nursing. In the past a back massage might be offered to relieve discomfort or help a patient rest without excessive pharmacological intervention. Today most patients would probably faint if offered a massage. Cleanliness is the best protection against disease. That's been a known fact for more than a century. With all the drug-resistant organisms out there, especially the hospital- acquired ones, the management at UHSB might want to rethink their priorities.

Unfortunately personal care is not likely to be on the roadmap of future healthcare. While advanced degrees are becoming more prevalent in the nursing field, the emphasis of nursing education is increasingly centered on leadership, research and the mastering of specialized high-tech equipment. Seminars and continuing education are often aimed at how to document your procedures so that you can avoid legal action. Nearly every Labor and Delivery nurse that I know has been involved in a legal action at some level, ranging from consulting with a hospital attorney to being a witness or defendant at a malpractice trial. In fact, the majority of a nurse's time is spent in documentation instead of at the bedside and the advent of computerized charting has only compounded the situation.

The burden of documentation often involves a plethora of ridiculous items cooked up by someone who obviously never spent time in a hospital caring for patients. While the intent is good, the process often leaves a lot to be desired. For example, there has been a much-needed initiative by JCOHA, the Joint Commission on Hospital Accreditation, to prevent wrong- site surgery. Since even one instance of removing the wrong foot or kidney or breast is way too many, the intention and merit of the initiative is definitely valid. Implementation of the initiative amounted to the creation of a "Time-out" prior to surgery during which everyone is supposed to stop what they are doing and come to an agreement as to who the patient is, what safety measures and consents have been obtained and, perhaps most important, what surgery is to be performed. All surgeons must be in the room and should not leave the room after the time out or I suppose they might be confused when they return and cut off the wrong leg. Whenever possible the patient should be involved in the identification process. I know that I wasn't in on the time-outs for my surgeries because the anesthesiologist put me to sleep before I even entered the operating room. Come to think of it, I'm probably lucky that I still have both kidneys! Actually maybe I should check for additional scars. I had so many drugs the first few days after surgery that I might not have noticed an extra bandage or two. As for the time-out process itself, the documentation has evolved into multiple checklists as well as double-charting on both paper and the computer. By the time I finish prepping the patient, counting the instruments and making sure that all the machines are hooked up and functioning properly, I often find myself looking up from the time-out checklist only to find out that the surgeons have already started. Luckily cesarean sections are pretty much the only surgery we do on my unit and there is usually only one uterus.

Chapter 14

Transfer to St. Charles

Getting back on my feet after the second operation proved to be more of a challenge than I had anticipated. My legs were severely weakened from both the spinal cord injury and the resultant weeks of inactivity. Drugs administered for pain relief probably contributed to my lack of coordination and I required a walker to ambulate around the circular hallway of the 18th floor.

The nurses blamed the high dose steroids for the frequent infiltration of my intravenous sites and the necessity for the incessant poking of my arms with needles. Both of my forearms were colored in a palette that ranged from deep purple to greenish yellow. The bruises ranged from my knuckles to my elbows and there were very few veins left to choose from. After a third unsuccessful attempt by my day nurse, I was told that the IV guru nurse had been summoned to replace my IV. "She never misses," I was assured. A short while later, the paragon entered the room with several other coworkers and I did a double take.

About three years before my illness, I hosted a pre-Christmas party at my home for a number of friends and family. It was a combination vendor party where a number of gifts could be purchased for the upcoming holidays. There was handmade jewelry sold by a friend-of-a-friend and knock-off pocketbooks that were amazing and trendy. But the funniest vendor at the party was in the business of selling, ehem, personal toys. The most popular toy was made famous on the TV show Sex and the City and the games and shenanigans of the vendor really made the party a hit. I remember her telling me that she was actually selling the products because she wanted money to go to nursing school. Yeah, okay. Just like the stripper at another friend's 40th birthday party was working her way through medical school. A likely story, right? Except that the guru of needles who had just come to start my IV for the gazillionth time was none other than the sex-toy Queen who had hosted my party! I guess dreams do come true...

Should I acknowledge our past acquaintance? Do her colleagues know? Is she still in the business? Will she be embarrassed? Will I?? I decided to reintroduce myself after she got the line in my arm. Of course she remembered me and my friends and we spent some time getting reacquainted. She has become a respected Professional Registered Nurse and I'm certain that I can't be the only patient who recognizes her. But apparently, to the disappointment of some of my friends, she no longer hosts sex-toy parties.

The Department of Physical Therapy continued to visit me each day to assist my use of the walker and observe my progress. Determined to speed my way back to health, I made a point of attempting to perambulate several times throughout the day, eventually proceeding as far as the bank of elevators. After my need for intravenous medications waned and I had progressed to oral pain medications, it was determined that I needed to be transferred within the week to another institution for rehabilitation. I missed my home and my cat but my life was no longer my own. Control over my destiny was out of the question. People who weren't paralyzed or on narcotics (one can only hope) were making all of my decisions for me. After my previous discharge, I had only been home for two days before returning to the hospital for my second operation. It seemed like home was still a distant objective.

The EMTs came for me at sundown, armed with a stretcher and several blankets to ward off the late February chill. While I had an idea that I would be moved to St. Charles Hospital for rehabilitation within a day or two, the appearance of my ride came suddenly and I felt like a tidal wave had come crashing down and was about to carry me away as staff members rapidly stuffed the accumulation of clothes and gifts into a large plastic bag. There had been no time or warning to pack and I hadn't had a chance to say goodbye to all of the staff members who had helped me. I was summarily herded to the stretcher by the social worker that had coordinated my displacement as she informed me not to worry; all of my stuff would be gathered for me. I suppose it was good that my egress was somewhat hurried. Who likes tearful goodbyes? But I hadn't yet consumed my daily fix of cheesecake…

The ride from Stony Brook University Hospital to St. Charles Hospital in Port Jefferson brought me a few miles closer to my home but I still had light years to travel in terms of regaining physical function. Thanks to the allowance of cell phones in hospitals I was able to inform family and friends of my whereabouts and thereby prevent them from sending out an APB. My roommate had preceded me to St. Charles a few days earlier and I looked forward to the possibility of seeing her again. Shortly after my arrival my nurse wheeled me out into the hallway for a surprise. My old roommate was waiting in her own two-wheeled carriage outside my room. It turned out that her sister was now my nurse and she wanted everyone to know how I had helped her when we were roommates back at Stony Brook. After a short reunion we were both ushered back to our respective rooms. I regret to say that I never saw her again despite the endless trips I made to physical therapy and, possibly due to the amount of drugs that were needed to keep me from crying out in pain, I don't remember her name. And sadly, I would come to wish that I never saw her sister the nurse again. She was probably the only professional that I met at Saint Charles Hospital that was less than stellar.

On the morning of my first full day at St. Charles Hospital I was given a schedule to follow containing all sorts of appointments for both physical and occupational therapy. It felt like going back to school again and, in a way, that's what it was. I had always been a good student and have a need to master whatever skill I set out to learn, so I undertook my assignments with the utmost concentration and vigor that a crippled body and a brain on pain meds could produce. The setup at St. Charles is very well thought out and most of the therapists are young, caring and enthusiastic. There is also a small recreational program and since I was eager for anything that would take my mind off of the pain and the fact that I was not able to work, I was wheeled off to the Occupational Therapy room on my first evening there to play a trivia game. Jeopardy had always been one of my favorite television shows, along with the Cash Cab (which I search for every time I go into New York City) so I thought I stood a fairly good chance of kicking ass and taking names. As we entered the room I was shocked to see a street curb complete with a pooch and a fire hydrant and a real car with doors ajar. It's a testament to the amount of drugs I had taken over the past few weeks by ingestion, injection and anesthesia that my first thought was that the car was the prize for winning the Jeopardy game. I actually vocalized this ludicrous thought and luckily the other contestants and the therapist running the game thought that I was making a funny. Or my next gig might well have been the psych ward. For those of you who are not familiar with rehabilitation gear, the car was there to teach people with certain disabilities the correct way to get in and out of a car. Having been through the ordeal with my father, who had sustained both a fractured hip and a stroke, I should have immediately understood that. My mind was obviously not up to par. In retrospect, considering the events of those weeks, the trauma and anesthesia and medications, it's amazing I have any recollections at all.

Over the next few weeks I progressed from using a walker to using a cane but my arms remained limp and useless from shoulder to elbow. This made for some interesting experiences while attempting to wash or dress myself. Pulling up my pants was a struggle that required determination and ingenuity. Applying underarm deodorant could be accomplished by grasping the lip of the sink and hanging on while I backed up. Then, by bending forward, I could bend my other arm at the elbow and just manage to reach the other armpit with the deodorant. I begged to be allowed to shower and was put off for another five days until the staples from my operating room "accident" were removed from my head.

At my urging, my daughter took a picture of my back and neck with my cell phone so that I could see the damage. Nearly ten days after the surgery, my upper back and neck were still horrifically swollen and bruised and covered with a foot-long row of steri-strips. My hair was a wretched mess, full of dried blood from the scalp laceration. Luckily I have a strong stomach but I feared for the health of my visitors and caretakers. I wanted a shower so bad that I would have sold my firstborn son to obtain one. It was a momentous occasion when I was finally escorted to the shower. This action actually required approval from the Occupational Therapist. She would also have to sign off in the future when I was ready to shower all by myself. For now, I was accompanied by a nursing assistant who walked behind me as I shuffled along with my walker. "You sure use a lot of hairspray." She noted in her lilting West Indian accent. Recalling the hair in the back of my head that was still stiff with dried blood more than a week after the operation, I could only stare at her. Even my inner voice was silent. I *never* use hairspray. And I'm certain that she figured that out shortly, when she washed my hair in the shower. The brown rivulets of old blood must have been a clue.

That first shower was better than any experience I can ever remember. People often use the superlative "better than sex". Well, this was. It was also better than chocolate, better than cheesecake, better than winning the lottery. Well actually I have never won the lottery so maybe it isn't fair to make that judgment. Let's just say it was really, really, really good. Psychologically it was like rejoining the human race. Being dirty is one of the most demoralizing and dehumanizing punishments heaped onto the sick and injured. As a nurse I've seen people at their worse. Toothless older men with grey stubble stained by the pureed crap they had been served for lunch. Sweat-stained women who have labored for days to give birth now covered in the fluids of childbirth. Underneath the persona viewed by the world are a handsome young man and a beautiful woman. But it's hard to start feeling better when you feel *dirty*.

The next day, after getting all sweaty again while climbing a flight of phony stairs in Physical Therapy, I wanted to relive the dream. I had a small toiletry bag full of wonderfully fragrant shower gels and shampoo and I was ready to rediscover the ecstasy of being clean once more. I was heartened to find that the nurse at the desk was the sister of my prior roommate from Stony Brook who had been so grateful for my help. After all, what goes around comes around, right? I approached the desk with alacrity and requested towels and permission to use the shower. My heart started skipping when she hedged, stating that there were no nursing assistants free today. After assuring her that I was quite capable of using the shower by myself despite the fact that I was still using a walker, I expected her to readily concede. Instead she looked down her rather long nose at me and stated, hand on hip, in a voice might have been reserved for a recalcitrant child, "You know, patients are not entitled to a shower *every* day."

I just stared back blankly. My inner voice was ranting away in overdrive and I could barely stand the din. *Entitled* can be a harsh word. I wasn't in prison and I hadn't committed a crime other than to have a lousy cervical spine. I so wanted to enquire if she had taken a shower that morning prior to coming to work. Or if she was only *entitled* to one every so often. Nurses don't realize the power of their words to a patient in distress. I will remember that moment for the rest of my life and I've told the story to hundreds of people. It was almost a caricature of how *not* to treat people. The indignity of not being allowed to have adequate personal hygiene is not a small thing. Think about the last time you became sweaty and grimy because of some undertaking, perhaps playing tennis in the heat of day or mowing the lawn or riding a horse or lying in the sand at the beach. And now you can't wait to take a shower. You can just imagine how good it's going to feel when you soap up and rinse off and your skin feels *clean* again. Now imagine someone telling you that you aren't allowed to shower. You have to remain dirty and repugnant even though all the people around you have showered. You are not worthy of taking a shower because you are a patient and therefore have no rights. You are not *entitled*.

I wanted to do evil things to her. But, nonviolent creature that I am, I simply retreated to my room to stew for a while. Then I stealthily crept out into the hall (as stealthy as you can be when you're shuffling along behind a walker), surreptitiously examined each closet and alcove that I passed until I located the towel stash. Grabbing a couple towels, I quickly folded them under my palms on the handle of the walker. Then, feeling like an action hero, I skulked into the nearest empty shower. My heart was pounding but nothing could stop me now. What could they do to me if they caught me? Turning on the shower was a challenge with my weakened arms and I nearly resorted to using my feet but eventually I managed the job. I had to stop a few times and sit down because my legs became wobbly. And I couldn't reach everywhere because of the limited movement of my arms. It was still the second most wonderful experience in my life.

Chapter 15

Homecoming

Reprimanded by the therapists whenever I was caught without my walker, I valiantly attempted to graduate to canehood but failed miserably. Walking with a cane requires a great deal of coordination and timing that I simply was not able to master. Somehow I managed to fake it enough to convince the staff that I was ready for discharge from St. Charles Hospital. Most of my stay there was dedicated to literally getting me back on my feet, with almost no attention paid to the fact that my upper arms were still completely paralyzed. My main goal was to go home where I would be in charge of my own destiny, such as being able to take as many showers as I wanted without subterfuge or begging for permission.

Since the only word thus far used in association with my leaving the hospital was the word "discharge", it was a shock to find that the plan was to send me to a nursing home. As in old people who wear diapers and don't know who they are. I used to joke that my kids would sign me over the first time I drooled or lost my car keys but this time it wasn't a joke. My Paramedic son had even scoped out the nursing homes on Long Island for me. I was amused to find out that some of them had bars and I quipped that I wanted to be put on the waiting list after he found out which homes served top shelf, had karaoke and kept the bar open the latest. Now it was a reality and I was no longer amused.

My main Physical Therapist and the Care Manager kept pointing out to me that due to the severity of my paralysis I could never take care of myself. My apartment was all on one floor but it was the *second* floor. I had managed to climb the phony flight of stairs in the rehab room so I didn't see the problem. After consulting with the Occupational Therapist, my son was prepared to move most of the dishes and glasses that I would need to the kitchen counters so that I could reach them. Cooking for myself might not render gourmet fare but I was confident that I could hustle up a PBJ on demand. And Peapod would fetch whatever I needed in the way of groceries. Deaf to my pleas and in spite of my despair the argument continued over several days while arrangements were initiated for nursing home placement. They simply refused to discharge me home as long as I lived alone.

Sparing me the final humiliation in my desperate hour of need, my dearest cousin Alicia stepped forward at the last moment and offered to move in with me until I was ready to fly solo. Several years my senior, she had been a veritable icon to me for as long as I could remember. She had taught me how to smoke and gotten me drunk for the first time. I followed her around like a puppy and stalked her when she had her first boyfriend. She taught me how to drive although she refuses to take the blame for my notorious lack of skill behind the wheel. Now we would be roommates. Her role in rescuing me from the fate of languishing in a nursing home is one of the most precious gifts anyone has ever given me.

Transportation was arranged via an ambulance since it was decided that I required assistance mounting the stairs. (I suppose that my performance on the phony stairs in Physical Therapy was not as stellar as I had thought?) Expecting a cold shoulder from my cat after such a long absence I was happily surprised to find her more affectionate than before I had left. It was mid-March and I had entered the hospital for my first surgery at the end of January.

The hypertension that I had acquired during my second Emergency Room admission delayed my home Physical Therapy for several weeks because the therapist would not work with me until my blood pressure was under control. I'm certain that the weight I had gained being a couch potato and enjoying the cheesecake at Stony Brook abetted the problem. Each day a visiting nurse would come to check my blood pressure and confer by telephone with my private physician, who would then juggle my medications. It was frustrating to watch the physical therapist shake her head with regret and leave because the numbers were still too high. I was so anxious to continue therapy and get back to my life. Finally, the numbers were acceptable enough to continue my Physical Therapy visits at home. I joked that other people pumped iron and I pumped aluminum when Daisy, my home Physical Therapist, had me lay on the bed and bench press my aluminum cane over my head. In the beginning she had to help me by supporting the cane with two fingers as I labored to lift it. Buoyed by the continual reassurance that nerve tissue takes up to a year and a half to heal I kept at it and made constant if slow progress.

Talking on the telephone for any length of time had always bothered my neck and the surgeries did not improve that result. With advisement from my son, I joined Facebook. I was so enamored with the forum that I proceeded to badger my friends at work to join and soon the phenomenon spread like wildfire. Within months my entire family as well as nearly everyone at work had joined and it is still a major form of communication (as well as a major time-suck) among my coworkers. For a shut-in like I had been forced to become, it was my digital conduit back to the human race.

After many weeks of in-home therapy I ditched my walker (I was never able to use the cane for anything more than a barbell) and my cousin was able to return home. I was now ready for outpatient therapy but still unable to drive so I was signed up for transportation and therapy at St. Charles hospital, this time in the outpatient department. It was heaven to get out of the apartment and it occurred to me that what I felt at the treat of witnessing the Earth come back to life that early spring must be akin to what a convict feels after release from a long prison sentence. My busmates and my physical therapists were pretty much the only regular contact I had with the outside world for the next few months and I enjoyed their company.

One of the unstated benefits of Physical Therapy is the need to get off of the couch and dress yourself, something that still took a good bit of effort. The extent of my paralysis at that time was such that in order to understand the extent of the difficulty in daily activities, you would have to secure your upper arms to your sides with a rope. Standing on my weakened legs for any length of time was equally difficult but I was lucky to have a large walk-in shower with a shower chair to sit on and my hand-held showerhead allowed me to stay clean. I dried my back by hanging a towel from the rack and rubbing my back against it. My hair was another matter. My neck was fused and had very little range of motion now. Even if I bent my head as far down as it would go, I couldn't reach the back of my head. I finally found a local Lemon Tree that would wash and blow-dry my hair for $15 every three or four days. A salon in my clubhouse and another a few blocks away charged $45 for the same service, a charge that I couldn't keep up with. My wardrobe now consisted of loose, stretchy pull-up pants, the only kind that I was able to manage, and loose tops with wide enough necks that I could bend my head into since I couldn't lift my arms to my head. Even so, it would take several minutes to work the pants up around my waste and struggle into my tops. Socks were donned with the aid of a nifty flat plastic invention that had two long straps to pull the sock up with after you loaded it on to the frame. Makeup wasn't an option; I simply lacked the coordination. By the time I made it to the street to catch the bus outside my door, I felt like I had already done an hour of calisthenics.

During my bus rides to the hospital I was entertained by my young driver who obviously suffered from a mood disorder. Frequent tales about his uncaring alcoholic father illustrated his disenchantment with the world. Even more entertaining were the escalating stories about his inharmonious relationship with his pregnant girlfriend. Perhaps it's a side effect of my personality as a nurse that relative strangers often share their problems with me. One day, the bus driver complained that his crazy girlfriend had locked him out because of something he had said and he had to spend the night sleeping outside on the picnic table. Insisting that it was not his fault and wanting my opinion to validate his position that she was in the wrong, he actually dialed her and put her on speakerphone so that I could hear their conversation. Cell phone usage while driving is known to be dangerous at any time. Driving a bus through a busy village and turning around to make eye contact with me over his girlfriends' responses was over the top and did not add to my sense of equilibrium that day.

Sheila, my Physical Therapist in the outpatient department at St. Charles Hospital and Karen, one of the assistants both stand out amidst a group of the most dedicated and talented health care workers that I have ever met. I give full credit for my continued recovery to them. My visits continued for nearly nine months, long after I had returned to work, but by mid-November I had used up the yearly supply of Physical Therapy visits that would be covered by my medical insurance.

Lucky for me I had rarely been sick before this illness and I didn't believe in gratuitously calling in sick. As a result I had been receiving full pay from a combination of sick time and vacation time for the entire tenure of my absence. This was about to change since my sick time was running out. I had been on a medical leave of absence for nearly six months. If I didn't return to work soon, I would have to start paying $500.00 a month to continue my medical insurance while no longer receiving a salary. And I needed medical insurance so that I could continue physical therapy. Sheila told me that I was crazy to even think about returning to work. I was still taking a considerable amount of narcotics to control the pain from constant spasms in my neck, upper back, shoulders and upper arms. My arms were still too weak and my gait was still uncoordinated. Worst of all, my neck was even more vulnerable to further injury because of the fusions and any strain could put me in severe jeopardy. I could end up completely paralyzed.

Chapter 16

Back to Work and Rejoining the World

For months I had been consuming a steady diet of narcotics that would have gained a good price on the streets. My physician and physical therapist did not think I should stop them because they tamped down the pain enough to enable me to continue moving and probably helped to keep my blood pressure under control. But if I was to go back to work, I needed to stop using them. Narcotic addiction and withdrawal is portrayed in hundreds of movies and television shows. And I had taken care of plenty of junkies when I worked in Manhattan. I wondered idly if I would experience all of the symptoms on the day that I eschewed my Oxycontin XL in lieu of Advil. I don't recall ever experiencing a high or feeling the least bit loopy while taking them, possibly because I wasn't opiate naïve due to all of the intravenous Dilaudid I had been given prior to starting on pills. Friends tell me now that I sometimes slurred on the telephone. The usual procedure when withdrawing from narcotics is to slowly wean off the drugs. Determined to free myself of the drugs in record time, and being a stubborn person, I went cold turkey.

I waited in vain for the sweats and the craziness that I had witnessed in others. They never came. The only symptom I ever got was severe diarrhea. No cramps or anything. Just water pouring out of me around the clock. I stayed hydrated as best I could and tried to prevent an electrolyte imbalance. After two weeks I had a doctors appointment and I imparted the information that I had gone cold turkey along with my symptoms. He looked at me and smiled wryly. "Oh you've got at least another week, maybe ten days of that," he said, "given the amount of medication you were on."

The next obstacle to overcome was getting back behind the wheel of a car. Luckily I was never a very good driver to begin with so my poor driving ability might not be as obvious as it would be in someone who had depth perception, for instance. The first time I decided to take the car out, the battery was dead. I guess that God was looking out for someone that day. By the time the mechanic came to charge the battery it was too late to drive. The second time I tried to drive, the battery was dead again. This is a car that was barely a year old and it had spent half of that year in a garage. Before he drove away for the second time in as many days, the tow truck guy advised me that I should not turn the car off for at least a half hour. Climbing into the car, I glanced at the dashboard and found that the yellow gas light was on. I was definitely going on a road trip, if only to the gas station! Pulling gingerly out of my driveway, I began my journey with a few circuits around my neighborhood. Having managed that without killing anyone, I struck out for the nearest gas station about a mile away. Luckily there were only two turns involved since turning the wheel involved much more skill than I remembered. (Try turning your steering wheel without using your upper arms and you'll understand what I mean.) I also wasn't able to turn my head before changing lanes or backing up. I couldn't adjust my rearview mirror because I couldn't reach it. I was able to lift my arms nearly waist high but there was still significant paralysis. As I drove onto the highway towards the gas station a mile or so away, it felt like the cars were whizzing by. I was always a relatively heavy-footed driver. So I was surprised when I looked down and discovered that I was barely doing 40. Along with my gimpy gait I had become the quintessential old lady driver. Somehow I made it to the gas station and filled my tank, apprehensive the whole time that the engine wouldn't turn back on. After leaving the gas station I rode up and down the highway near my home, relishing the freedom of being out and back in the world again.

I suppose I have learned what it is like to be seriously short, er, I mean vertically challenged. My son solved several of my problems when he came down from Boston the following week. First he adjusted the rearview mirror with me sitting in the drivers seat. Then he applied tiny convex mirrors to the surface of my sideview mirrors to minimize the blind spots and reduce the danger that stemmed from my inability to turn my head. Before long I was driving further afield each day. The commute to my job was about thirty-five minutes long. I had to work up the stamina to drive that distance and still be able to work for thirteen hours.

My fingers still lacked my pre-illness coordination but the stiffness that I had experienced throughout my illness was nearly gone so I was able to type relatively well. It had been nearly four weeks since I had weaned myself off of narcotics and I had driven further each day. Definite progress toward my goal of returning to work, but I still couldn't lift my arms more than a few inches from my side. My neurosurgeon had given me a ten pound weight limit for lifting and I often needed to lay down after performing nearly any task that lasted more than an hour because of painful spasms in my neck and upper back. I decided to contact my director and find out if I could come back to work in an alternate position until I was able to perform the very physical job of nursing in Labor and Delivery. In addition to involving long hours on my feet, the job requires a good deal of upper body strength including the ability to lift occasionally heavy legs, dead weight due to the effects of epidural anesthesia, into and out of stirrups as well as pushing an occasional stretcher and even giving suprapubic pressure in the event of a newborn shoulder becoming trapped in the pelvis. Stubborn as a mule when told that I can't do something, even I had to admit that I was not up to these tasks.

Several friends had called and urged me to inquire about other jobs that they had heard of. Supposedly someone from Human Resources had been on my unit and spoken of jobs that would be perfect for me. Another friend had left a few years earlier and was working in the computer charting section for the entire Catholic Healthcare System and it was rumored that there might be a job there. Definite prospects. My CV included experience in lecturing and authorship on both a broad and local level. I had contributed to an EMT textbook and lectured to small and large audiences alike. I had written many of the policies and procedures in our manuals and trained many of my colleagues.

I called the Director of Maternal Child Health who had hired me thirty-one years before to see if I could come back to work but temporarily perform different tasks such as precepting new nurses. I could do part of an admission such as take a history, type and do paperwork but there were some things, even some simple tasks such as hanging an IV bag from a pole that were simply beyond me at the time. Surely there were things that I could do until my arms started to work again. After a very brief hesitation she informed me that not only was there no such thing as "light duty", my six month leave of absence was nearly over and she couldn't hold my job indefinitely. A call to Human Resources brought further bad news: my sick and vacation time ran out the following week. The hospital would begin to charge me the five hundred dollars a month for medical benefits if I didn't return to work the following week. And my salary was about to stop. How would I survive?

I contacted my friend in the computer charting section only to find out that the job had already been filled. Another would be coming up within a year or so and she would keep me in mind but I needed a job, and healthcare benefits, now. Physical therapy visits were vital to my recovery and I could never afford to continue if I had to pay for them without insurance. In desperation I contacted Human Resources for a job. The only full time position available was in Care Management. They preferred someone with experience in that field and I would have to apply for the job. There was no guarantee that I would get it. After thirty-five years as a nurse I was suddenly unmarketable in the midst of the biggest recession in decades. The word "homeless" began to float around inside my skull and I began to have difficulty sleeping.

My friends egged me on with claims that the hospital couldn't fire me. Weren't there laws that protected the rights of handicapped people? This was a Catholic hospital for crying out loud! The hospital motto was "Our mission is caring". Could they really fire me? I spoke with another friend who is an attorney. Yes, they could fire me. They weren't saying that they wouldn't hire a handicapped person. I was quite welcome to apply for another job within my physical limitations that might pay minimum wage but they were well within their rights to terminate my employment if I was no longer able to perform the job they hired me for.

After ruminating over the subject for several days I phoned my nurse manager to tell her I was coming back to work. Shocked, she stammered out an inquiry as to the state of my health. "I'm fine," I replied. Employee Health would require a note from my physician stating that I was fit to return to work. (Show me a nurse who can't get a doctor's note that states just about anything and I'll sell you the Brooklyn Bridge!)

My physical therapist was adamantly against my returning to work. Convinced that my condition warranted permanent disability and that I would injure myself irreversibly if I returned to work, she urged me to reconsider. When I developed symptoms in C7, the vertebrae just below the four that were fused, she refused to continue therapy until I was cleared by my neurosurgeon. Alarmed, I made an immediate appointment. He perused my recent films and shook his head before turning back to me. "I can't turn you into a lollipop," he said. It took a moment for me to understand. If he fused any more of my spine I would walk around like Lurch from the Adams Family, completely unable to turn my head. He prescribed an additional anti-inflammatory and advised me to return in a couple of months.

With thirteen-hour shifts, full time employees work three days a week. I would still have enough days off to continue the Physical Therapy that was paramount to my continued recovery. The downside, of course, was that they were thirteen-hour shifts. The night before I returned to work for the first time was sleepless and terrifying. Was I out of my mind? What would my reception be? How could I possibly get through the day? There was only one way to find out.

The first day was a revelation in how great my friends are and the first few weeks were torture but as I continued to heal I realized that coming back to work was one of the best therapies I could have undergone. I was forced to perform movements that woke up my atrophied arm muscles and, more importantly, I rejoined the world. My coworkers in the Delivery Room were and continue to be angels in their willingness to help me with the tasks that are beyond my physical ability. They've got my back and the feeling is both humbling and uplifting. Not that there weren't a few close calls. The first time I carried a baby down the hall after returning to work could have ended in disaster. As I said, my neurosurgeon had given me a ten-pound weight lifting limit. This baby was probably a little over eight pounds. I started down the hall toward the infant transporter cradling the newborn close to my body while the proud father walked directly behind me. An eight-pound weight to me at that time was probably equivalent to a healthy woman carrying close to a hundred pounds. By the time I got halfway there, my arms began to tremble and I feared that I wouldn't be able to make it. I couldn't just drop this baby but my arms were cramping and the thirty feet between the transporter and me suddenly seemed more like thirty miles. Luckily, at that time, another nurse came out of a room, looked at me and immediately understood my distress. My eyes must have telepathed my panic and I imagine that my complexion must have resembled a bowl of flour. Without alerting the father as to the peril his newborn child was in, she grabbed the infant transporter and brought it to me, wresting the baby from my arms in the nick of time. For a long while after that, I would bring the transporter to the room instead of carrying the infant down the hall. And then I would ask the father of the baby to lift the newborn into the warmer, a practice that made him feel special anyway. Much of my reintegration at work involved an almost seamless series of traded tasks. I could start IVs but couldn't actually hang the IV bag up on the pole. So hang my bags and I'll start your IVs.

My first post-surgical swim in a pool was groundbreaking. For the first time, with the added buoyancy of the water, I was able to lift my arms to shoulder height. Excited with my new achievement, I began to do pool exercises the rest of the summer. I still wonder why water isn't used more often as a physical therapy adjunct. I might never have regained as much function if I hadn't lived in a place that had a swimming pool.

Water can also be deadly. In another water incident a year later, I nearly drowned. My children and I had gone to one of the south shore ocean beaches on the Forth of July, hoping to spend the day at the beach and then enjoy fireworks. I had grown up on Long Island and used to be a pretty strong swimmer. "Used to be" is the key operative phrase here. To this day I forget that I have weaknesses because in my mind I picture myself being able to do anything that I used to do. I went for a swim with my kids and my son-in-law early in the day and had no problem. Then after dinner I decided to return for another refreshing dip. No one was interested in joining me. Youth is wasted on the young! So I headed into the surf alone and mostly did my strange lopsided arms-in-the-water backstroke that I had perfected since my surgery since I could no longer do a freestyle stroke.

The surf had become rougher since the morning and there was a slight undertow so after jumping a few waves I decided to get out before I got too tired. When I was nearly clear of the surf a wave rolled in, knocked me down into the sand and tossed me around like laundry on a spin cycle. I know better than to fight the ocean so I went limp and waited for it to let go of me before I tried to get up. It still takes me a moment to get up from my knees if I'm on all fours due to residual weakness, even if I haven't been recently flattened by a wave. Before I could rise, a second wave knocked me flat again and spun me in circles. The third wave caught me before I even made it to my knees. Before number four fully receded the fifth wave ground my jaw into the hardened sand and I could barely get my arms under me for a new attempt to get to my knees. By the sixth wave I was reduced to gasping for enough breath to sustain me through the next wave. I was exhausted and starting to consider the reality that I might drown in a foot of water because I didn't have the strength to stand up. Suddenly I felt strong hands grasp my arms and lift me to my feet. They dragged me out of the surf and held me upright until I could balance on my own two legs. The next day I could catalog where they held me by the blue fingerprints on my upper arms. They were a painful accompaniment to the egg on the back of my head that I must have gotten when I was pounded against the unforgiving sand. One of my rescuers still clung tight to my arm and started to urge me toward the first aid station. She claimed to be a doctor from Mount Sinai Hospital. I was dazed and weak and I wanted nothing more than to return to my beach chair, get my head together and sift through the knowledge that I was still alive. She naturally assumed that I was stinking drunk. Why else would someone wallow in a foot of water and not be able to get up from their knees? Continuing to resist her pleas to head over to first aid, I returned to my chair and found my son fast asleep on the blankets. It took several moments for the world to stop spinning and my heart to slow down. Just as my breathing was returning to normal, I looked up to find four beach cops standing over me.

"Ma'am you have to leave now," said the one closest to me.

I looked up in bewilderment. What the hell?

"You've been drinking and you have to leave."

"What are you talking about? I'm fine." I responded, slowly realizing that the Park Police had been sent over by Mount Sinai Doctor Lady.

As a unit they stiffened and formed a semi-circle around me in my little beach chair in the sand. Then the leader said, "You can make this easy or you can make it hard."

Jeez. I know cops. As dizzy as I had been a few moments ago, I could tell that this guy would love to use his handcuffs on me. It was their job to keep the beach free of drunks on the Forth of July and they believed that they had found a drunk. I woke my son and asked where my daughter and son-in-law had gone. Turned out they wanted to leave and had gone to get the car. My son was a little confused to wake up to a gaggle of park police but rose and helped to gather our things. They wouldn't even let us exit from the main entrance. We were ushered directly up the dunes and onto the sidewalk and then marched to the traffic circle. "Are you intending to drive Ma'am?" first cop asked. He was nearly salivating at the possibility of adding another DUI notch to his belt.

"No. My son-in-law went to get the car."

"Can you call him on your cell phone?"

"No. It's in my purse in the trunk of the car. That he went to get."

It was another mortifying fifteen minutes before my daughter and son-in-law arrived with the car. My son-in-law raised his eyebrow when he took in the situation and smiled. This was a seriously entertaining scenario: his mother-in-law being ejected from the beach and held hostage by four park police due to supposed public drunkenness.

"Depraved!" he whispered to me as we entered the car. He would have fun with this one for years to come!

I still have back and neck pain that accompanies the occasional moments of difficulty and disappointment when I realize that I can't and may never do something again that I was able to do *before*. I still don't know if I can ski or play tennis but I hope to find out one of these days. My "anesthesia brain" finally reversed after several years and I can once again concentrate enough to read several books at a time without my mind wandering into outer space. My neurosurgeon told me I can never ride a horse again and I find that depressing because horses were such a sweet part of my life. But less than a year after my hospital discharge I was painting again and I attended my first solo art show in a gallery on the North Fork of Long Island. The first time my work was shown at the gallery, I was in the hospital and couldn't attend. My son went to the gallery and had his picture taken next to my painting so I could see it hanging on the wall.

I can now lift my arms over my head and hang my own IV bags if the hook isn't too high. A personal trainer got me back on the treadmill and last summer I relearned how to ride a bicycle. If I ever feel a whining fit come on, my inner voice pipes up and reminds me that not too long ago I was paralyzed with no clue as to what was wrong with me. I raise my once-deadened arms above my head and glory in the knowledge that I'm still independent in every way and working full time as a nurse while enjoying a full second life as an artist. I faced total disability head-on and, with the help of my family, friends and some dedicated medical professionals, I came out the other side. If I can survive that, I can take on anything. Well, I probably won't go swimming alone in the ocean again.

Being on the other side of the siderail was devastating and demeaning because it stripped me of every defense, everything I had ever been proud of or cocky about. I was totally helpless, naked and at the mercy of my caregivers. But for the same reasons, it was also a gift. When I was in nursing school we used to talk about adding a class where everyone had to actually be a patient for an entire day. Use a bedpan. Have a foley catheter inserted in your urethra. Get poked and prodded by strangers who have a less than perfect understanding of the fact that you don't appreciate sharing your nakedness with the world. Have to wait all day for the decision of whether your day as a patient was over or would you have to remain helpless in bed for an undetermined amount of time. Not being allowed to eat or drink or get out of bed for an undetermined amount of time.

Nothing brings home the horror and the fear of what a patient must endure as well as living it yourself. Nursing education has gravitated more and more into the arena of theory and rhetoric. Perhaps it's time to put down the clipboards and the computers and bring the training of nurses and the practice of nursing back to the simple acts of relieving pain and suffering for a scared and suffering human being. Maybe every nurse and every doctor needs to spend some time on the other side of the siderail.

Acknowledgements

Surviving a life changing illness alone is probably possible but I'm glad I didn't have to find out how difficult it would have been. I received hundreds of cards and phone calls that kept me from feeling isolated. My daughter Tara Stapleton-Downes was a rock who was always there for me despite the fact that she lives and works in another state. Knowing that someone will be there when you wake from surgery is one more reason to pull through in the first place. Her grounded strength and outlook kept me sane when I wanted to fall apart. My son Edward Stapleton III was also living in another state at the time but managed to brighten my bedside and lift my spirits with his quirky sense of humor that mirrors my own. He was also invaluable with formatting advice in the creation of this book. My dear friends Linda Semcken and Esther Amsterdam had heavy loads of their own to carry but somehow managed to keep me grounded and make the trek to the North Shore to pop in on me when I needed it the most. They are my heroes; the Registered Nurses that you wish were taking care of you. My cousin Alicia has my undying gratitude for keeping me out of a nursing home. She was my heroine from childhood who became my savior as an adult. Last I want to thank my Mom and Dad, Grace and Joe Bartolillo. Mom was a

WAC during WWII in the medical corp. I've never known anyone so caring, brave and true and I miss her every day. And my Dad was the other half of the couple who all my cousins wished were their parents. He had his own trials with hospitals and is finally free from his wheelchair and making beautiful things in heaven.

CPSIA information can be obtained at www.ICGtesting.com
Printed in the USA
LVOW12s1849200214

374552LV00002B/466/P